More Play Helps

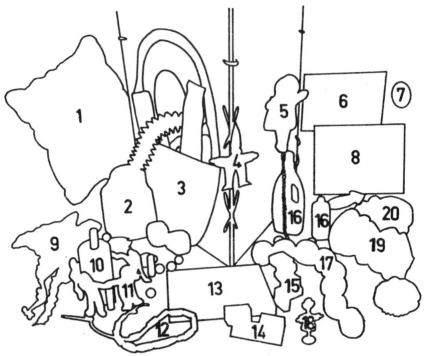

Key:

MORE PLAY HELPS
Play Ideas for Children
with Special Needs

ROMA LEAR

HEINEMANN MEDICAL BOOKS

Heinemann Medical Books
An imprint of Heinemann Professional Publishing Ltd
Halley Court, Jordan Hill, Oxford OX2 8EJ

OXFORD   LONDON   SINGAPORE   NAIROBI
IBADAN   KINGSTON

First published 1990

British Library Cataloguing in Publication Data
Lear, Roma
More play helps: play ideas for children
with special needs
1. Toys for handicapped children. Making.
I. Title
745.592

ISBN 0 433 00106 2

Phototypeset by Wilmaset, Birkenhead, Wirral
Printed and bound in Great Britain by
Courier International,
at Tiptree, Essex

Contents

Acknowledgements

My grateful thanks go to –

all the people who have contributed their ideas to this book; without their help and ready cooperation, it would never have been written.

Anita Jackson and Stuart Wynn-Jones for their delightful illustrations;

Gillian Hunter and Caroline Gould for additional pictures from *Play Helps*;

Michael Southgate for the cover picture;

Deborah Jaffé for checking the Appendices;

Gwen Holden for her help with the typing;

Florina Zutter for putting me in touch with all the contributors from Switzerland;

the Staff at *Play Matters* and my friends in toy libraries for their encouragement and support;

and, particularly, to my husband John, who has acted as critic and sounding board throughout the writing of this book.

Foreword

No one can spend more than five minutes in Roma Lear's company and fail to notice two things: one is her expertise in creating stimulating, interesting toys from everyday objects and the other is her extraordinary capacity to transmit her bubbling enthusiasm, ideas and skills to all those aroundher.

These two qualities are bonded together by her genuine humanity and commitment to giving children, often with very profound handicaps, a better quality of leisure experience and the opportunities, through play, to realise their full potential.

The National Toy Libraries Association owes Roma, who started one of the very first toy libraries twenty years ago, a great debt. She has become a source of inspiration to succeeding generations of toy librarians. Not only have her home-made toys become the catalyst for people's new creative ideas but, additionally, the principle underlying her toy making is recognised and accepted by all good practitioners.

The *process of play* is far more important than the toys. Parents and all practitioners working with children know that play is a child's work, through which they gain knowledge of themselves and their world. The enjoyment, the excitement, the pride of achievement when new skills are mastered as the toys are used, and above all the quality of the interaction between adult and child are the real benefits.

The toys suggested in this book are not made to last a life time. They are short-term toys for a particular situation; a specific child. Neither are they untried and tested. They spring from the real world of children's special needs rooted as they are in keen observation of children playing, a clear understanding of child development, and an extensive knowledge of disabilities and handicaps.

More Play Helps will be an invaluable and informative guide for toy librarians, parents and child care practitioners searching for inexpensive and quickly made toys and activities to suit children who may require out of the ordinary play materials.

It is typical of Roma's generosity that the royalties for this book will be given to *Play Matters* / The National Toy Libraries Association to develop our work with children with special needs.

Glenys Carter
Director
Play Matters/NTLA

Introduction

Isn't it strange how often bright ideas seem to come in the middle of the night? I was attending the International Conference of Toy Libraries at Toronto in the Summer of 1987 and, on the night in question, it was far too hot to sleep. My mind was busy with the events of the day, relating them to the toy library at Kingston-upon-Thames, which was my particular concern at the time, and to the needs of some of our more problematical members. Many people attending the Conference shared my interest in trying to find just the right toys to please children who, because of their particular handicaps, found that commercial ones had only limited appeal. In the way of thoughts in the early hours of the morning, mine turned this way and that, reminding me of all the parents, teachers, therapists and toy librarians I had met since the first publication of *Play Helps* in 1977. This current book might well have been called 'Play Helps – The Feedback', for it occurred to me that I could spend the first few years of my retirement asking around for other people's ideas, collecting them into 'More Play Helps' for children with very specialised needs, be they physical, mental or a mixture of both. All the thoughts in the proposed book would be there to be shared. People could dip into it, as with *Play Helps*, and hopefully they would find *something* which both they and the children would enjoy. If it also helped their development, so much the better.

I decided to collect only home-made ideas. Bought toys have an important part to play in the development of any child and in providing him with happy activity. Unfortunately, not everyone has access to a toy library or good toy shop – or the money or space required. Designs change and, in a book such as this, by the time it reaches print, the toy suggested may be unobtainable. How much more sensible to suggest DIY ideas which can easily be adapted to meet the needs of a particular child. With a little thought, almost anything can be made heavier or lighter, larger or smaller, easier or more complicated, and even given the right colour to give it individual child appeal.

I began on my home patch and, armed with a brand new notebook, collected ideas from our toy library parents and from all the therapists and teachers of children with special needs in our area. I wrote to friends from around the world who had attended the Conference in Toronto. As the months passed, when I attended toy library functions, schools, playgroups, parents' meetings etc., talking about the ideas in *Play Helps*, I would ask for contributions to its sequel. The response was encouraging.

I wanted ideas which were in the low technology bracket, and needed only normal skills to carry them out. Gradually, all the suggestions grouped themselves into three categories: *Instant*, could be done at once, providing you had the raw materials; *Quick*, could be made by anyone who was prepared to take a little trouble; and *Long-lasting*, needing some needlework or carpentry skills to make a sturdy and child-resistant job.

The problem of classifying all the ideas was a weighty one. The children needing them might be severely handicapped in one or many ways – perhaps physically, mentally, emotionally, or any combination of all three. The new collection of toys and activities would not sort themselves conveniently under the five senses as in *Play Helps*, so that format could no longer be used. The next obvious choice was to see how the letters of the alphabet could be applied. Allowing for a little jiggery pokery, such as R for Rock and Roll and Xtra Odds and Ends for X, Y, Z, this plan seemed to work well enough. Some letters head a collection of several ideas, other sections are shorter. Here and there are a selection of 'one liners'; clever ideas which may be just what you wish you had thought of yourself!

In no way is this book intended to be a plan for structured or therapeutic play. It is meant to be dipped into, not read from cover to cover in an orderly way. It is a patchwork of ideas and helpful hints, some original, some traditional, but all relevant to *someone* with special needs. All the ideas are attributed to their originators, except in the case of the 'one liners'. Whether you are a parent, therapist, teacher, nurse, carer, relative or friend, I am sure all the contributors to this book join me in hoping you will find many useful and entertaining ideas, which will help to bring more happiness to the children.

March, 1990   Roma Lear

Part I

CREATING THE CONDITIONS
FOR PLAY

WAYS OF
HANGING TOYS

MAKING IT POSSIBLE TO PLAY

Everyone caring for children with special needs will
know how difficult it can be to keep playthings within
reach of the child who needs them – and, occasionally,
out of reach of the one who doesn't! All children who, for
whatever reason, are unable to choose and fetch their
own toys need help to be able to play. Cot and pram toys
are easily bought for babies who are simply too young to
have learnt to be mobile, but for those older children
who are still confined to a cot (or its equivalent) because
of their disabilities, such toys may neither appeal nor be
appropriate. They will need their own special playthings
made into a cot toy suitable just for them. There are
many children who are able to sit up, but because of
their young age or handicap are still unable to move. If
given toys to hold, they are sure to drop them. Even if the
toys remain within reach, they may be unwilling or
unable to search for them. Many children have jerky,
uncoordinated movements. Without help, their toys are
soon swept to the floor or knocked out of reach. What
about 'frail' children? They may be able to move, but in
order to save them effort, their play materials need
organising in the most convenient way. Other children
may be temporarily incapacitated, like the toddlers on
traction for whom the train cushion on p. 13 was
specially designed. And so the list goes on.

Many people have thought up ingenious ways of
solving these problems. Simple ideas, though elusive,
are often the most effective. Perhaps someone else's

3

brainwave is just what you wish you had thought of yourself! The advantage of any 'do it yourself' solution is that there is room for adaptation and ingenuity. Everything can be simplified or developed to suit individual requirements. It's the *idea* that is important. If your child has difficulty in reaching or retaining his toys, read on. Help could well be among the tried and tested ideas that follow.

For children who are lying down

Use an Elastic Luggage Strap

Instant

This has strong hooks at both ends and can be hung across the cot so that the baby can reach the toys that dangle from it. It can be easily removed when the cot side needs lowering. It should be *slightly* stretched between the cot rails to prevent it sagging in the middle, so it is wise to measure before buying. Hang some toys with string or tape, but use elastic for others, so that when they are pulled and released they will bob about.

Use a Broomstick

Quick

Susan Harvey,
'Play in Hospital'

Cut a broomstick to the right size to straddle the cot bars comfortably. To make sure there is no danger of it falling on to the child, one end must be notched, so that it is located securely over one top rail, and the other end must be fixed to the opposite rail. A strong rubber band is suitable for the job and is easy to remove when the child needs attention. Push the broomstick through the rubber band, so that it goes *over* the broomstick, *under* the cot rail and back *over* the end of the broomstick. Cut a few grooves along the top of the broomstick to stop the strings attached to the hanging toys from sliding about and bunching together.

WAYS OF KEEPING TOYS TO HAND

Three Unusual Toy Holders

All Instant

The Sense Centre for Deaf/ Blind Children

There are many disabled children, particularly those with a visual handicap, who need to have their toys kept in a special place so that they can learn to find them easily. Teachers of deaf/blind children at the Sense Centre suggest three ways of helping to solve the lost toy problem by tying toys to a portable base.

1. The first idea is to use a plastic sink mat, obtainable from a hardware shop. Its normal function is to stop the washing-up bowl from scratching the sink, but the grid pattern of holes in the plastic makes it an ideal toy holder. It is both washable and tough. The toys can be spaced out and hung from fairly short lengths of tape or string to prevent them from tangling or becoming entwined in the child's hands.

2. You could go for something even more unusual and use a shelf from the oven!

3. The third suggestion is to use a plastic (or plasticised wire) draining tray, also from the hardware shop, and usually to be found on the draining board, loaded up with freshly washed plates and cutlery. Because of all the curved racks and recesses, this idea could be specially appealing to the exploring fingers of a visually handicapped child.

All these ideas can be used tied to the bars of a cot. If the child can move about, a toy holder with all its bits and bobs attached can be anchored to a certain spot in the room where the child can always find it – e.g. to the back of an upright chair. It can also be taken into the car (or school coach), but for some children its chief attraction will be that it can be *carried around*.

MORE PLAY HELPS

Playing on a Sloping Surface

Instant

Pam Courtney,
Deputy Head Teacher,
St Anne's School

A profoundly handicapped child is sure to have great difficulty in keeping his toys within reach, for he may have very limited controlled movement and may well have poor sight and hearing as well. It is not surprising that a child with all these problems may soon lose interest in his play. If he pushes his toys away with an involuntary movement, there they will stay – out of reach – out of sight – and out of mind. The child is left with nothing to do until someone notices his plight.

Pam has suggested a way in which this situation can be improved. If the child is playing on the floor, lying on one side, a sheet of hardboard can be placed between him and the wall, and the far edge of this board can be raised, so that when toys are pushed away, they will slide down and back to him.

For a *small* child who is able to sit up, a baby bath with one end slightly raised has been used with success. (Prop it up on the telephone directory!) The high sides of the bath also help to keep the toys to hand. Pam has found that for some children it is better to put plenty of toys in the bath, not just one or two. This way the child is more likely to notice them. He may possibly make a choice, and be tempted to investigate and play. As an alternative to the bath 'child and toy container', you could use a plastic, oval laundry basket. This has the added advantage that toys can be strung across it or tied to the sides – useful if the child would otherwise end up sitting on most of them!

A Play Necklace to Use With a Baby

Instant

R.L.

Everyone used to nursing babies knows how they love to grab at ear-rings, glasses, or a beard. If your baby is at this stage, it is easy to turn this spontaneous and delightful play into something much less painful, and possibly expensive, simply by adorning yourself with a *play* necklace. All you need is a loop of material which is comfortable for you to wear, perhaps use an old scarf or stocking, or even a strip of material. To this, at intervals, tie all sorts of suitable 'excitements' such as rattles, teethers or anything that takes your fancy from the list on p. 55. Sit your baby on your knee, facing you. Cradle him in your arms, supporting his head in your hands and settle down to enjoy all the eye contact and fun you will have together.

A Table Top Necklace

Quick

Mrs Crane,
The Manor School

Tying toys to a necklace for a *child* to wear is obviously not a good idea, because of the risk of it tightening around his neck. But to make a string of playthings which can be looped over a table top can be another option in the search for ways to keep toys within reach of the child who needs them, and out of reach of those who don't!

The first table necklace was made, in desperation, by a teacher at a school for children with severe learning difficulties. In her group were several lively lads, and one who was unable to move about. This boy was quiet and gentle. His favourite occupation was to shake and rattle plastic toys. Unfortunately, his class mates often took a fancy to his playthings and grabbed them from him, leaving him very upset. (Naturally!) His teacher came up with an answer. She collected all his favourite toys and tied each to the middle of a strip of nylon tape. She cut three more pieces of the same tape, each twice as long as the width of his play table, with plenty of 'extra for luck'. She plaited these together and, at intervals, both ends of the tape with a toy attached were incorporated into the plait. This long 'necklace' was laid across the table top and passed under it so that the ends could be knotted together to make a loop. The boy could now sit at the table and pull on the necklace until he reached the toy of his choice. He was able to enjoy his favourite activity in uninterrupted peace.

Materials
- Long lengths of nylon tape, or rug wool, or macramé twine, or even strips of material. Use double if you want a fat plait.
- Shorter lengths of tape to tie on each toy.
- A selection of toys. The original table necklace had 'Flip Fingers', a large plastic ring, a plastic car, a pair of plastic scissors, a trainer ball with holes in it, a string of large beads, keys and various rattles.

A Roller Doodle Loop

Quick

R.L.

The idea of making a doodle toy on the principle of a roller towel was sparked off by the success of the table necklace. Such a toy turned out to be a convenient way of providing some temporary amusement for children in a hospital ward where most were in wheelchairs.

Perhaps they were just back from swimming or school, but with only half an hour to wait before lunch, it was impractical for busy nurses to give out toys. To try to meet the need for a simple activity to fill this gap, a series of loops of material (like miniature roller towels) were made, and then suitably embellished. These could slide over the trays of the wheelchairs. A box full of these doodle loops was kept in the ward office. Because of the generous supply, the children were unlikely to be given the same one twice running, so they were eager to explore their one for the day.

Materials

- A piece of material about 300 mm wide and long enough to loop loosely round the tray of a wheel-chair.
- Suitable embellishments! Before joining the material into a loop, decorate it as you fancy. When inspiration deserted me, I just stitched on a patchwork of materials of different colours and textures. In my more creative moments, I sewed on fur fabric teddy bears, boats of PVC floating on a sea of ric-rac ripples, flower shapes with button centres, houses with doors and windows to open and, of course, loops of tape were included here and there so that rattles and other toys could be attached. People who are fond of sewing will find more ideas in the 'Buttons and Bows' section, p. 43.

Use a Cake Icing Turntable

Instant

Alison Wisbeach,
Head Occupational Therapist,
The Wolfson Centre

An immobile child whose reach is restricted in any way, may have to put up with the frustration of only having a tiny play area she can touch. Try tucking your elbows into your sides and keep them there while you carry out a simple task like writing a letter, putting it in the envelope and sticking on the stamp, and the problem becomes plain. It is possible to extend the reach of a child in this situation by putting her toys on a revolving cake turntable. Imagine a child in a wheelchair with one of these gadgets on her tray. Perhaps she wants to play with doll's house furniture. Easy! Divide the turntable into four with two strips of cardboard the same width as the diameter. Slot these together to make a cross and instantly the child has four rooms she can fill as she wishes. When one is finished to her satisfaction, she can rotate the turntable and start on the next.

Use a Revolving Play Tidy

Long-lasting

Karen Padgett Chandler, Hospital Play Specialist

Think of a cake turntable with containers of different sizes fixed to it and you will understand the principle behind this useful play tidy.

The prototype was specially designed to make play easier for a group of four children sharing activities at a drawing table while waiting for their turn for treatment at a Hospital Out-Patients' Department. The containers held paper, pencils, felt pens, sticky shapes, scissors etc. The revolving top of the play tidy made sure these were within *easy reach* of everyone. It is this last feature which could make a revolving play tidy a boon to many immobile children.

The play tidy consists of two basic parts: a circular rotating top with a variety of containers screwed to it, and a square wooden base fitted with non-slip rubber feet. The containers should be different sizes and shapes. Use various plastic boxes, tins with safe rounded edges, a sink tidy etc. Make sure the top is larger than the base. It must overhang so that it is easy to rotate without squashing small fingers.

Materials
- A square wooden base
- Four non-slip rubber feet
- A circular wooden top, with a hole in the middle for the screw
- A long screw and a washer to join the top to the base
- A variety of containers to screw to the top

A Train Cushion

Long-lasting

Designed by Jean Gregg, Made by Sarah Bondoux, Play Specialists, Lord Mayor Treloar Hospital

This delightful play cushion was specially designed to meet the particular needs of small children on abduction frames in a hospital ward. Their legs and hips were immobilised, but their hands were free to play with anything they could reach. The cushion acted as a toy holder. It was stuffed with an oblong of plastic foam which made it rigid enough to stand at the side of the cot to form a cosy play corner and hide the child from the rest of the ward. The play leaders thought this was an important point. Children love to creep into a hidey hole now and then, to 'get away from it all'. Fixed to an abduction frame in a busy hospital ward there is no chance of a quiet play under the dining room table! The train cushion was tied to the cot bars to give the illusion of privacy and helped to fill this need.

The appliqued picture on the cover was the part that attracted the children. Across the middle steamed a train towing three carriages. Each colourful felt carriage made

a pocket in which small toys, dolls, finger puppets, crayons etc. could be stored. The lucky child having her turn with the cushion could easily help herself to what she wanted. A plume of 'steam' came from the funnel. This was made from a strip of swansdown, flowing up from the funnel and along the top of the cushion. It was stitched down securely along its entire length. (Not everyone has swansdown in their bits bag! Ric-rac braid could make a poor substitute!)

Apart from its special function of making play possible for the bed-bound children, the cushion could also be propped against the playroom wall, or used flat on the floor. It was a delight to look at, and when not being played with made an attractive nursery picture.

Materials
- A block of plastic foam, which conforms to British Safety Standards; size approximately 900 x 750 x 100 mm.
- Material for the cover. The prototype was pale blue.

This contrasted well with the stong colours used for the train.

- Scraps of bright material for the train and carriages. Felt is colourful and easy to use, but it does not wash well. It is better to use woven material, if the cushion is likely to need disinfecting, or have heavy use.
- Black material for the funnel and wheels (or use buttons for these).
- Swansdown (optional extra!) for the steam.
- Zip-fastener (optional).

Method

From the cover material, cut two oblongs the same size as your foam block. These make the front and back of the cover. This needs to fit snugly to avoid creases, so do not allow extra for seam turnings. Cut a long strip of cover material, the same width as the foam block and long enough to go all round the edge with 'a little bit for luck' for the final seam. This strip, of course, makes the gusset which later joins the front to the back. Next, design the front of the cushion. The easiest way is to draw the train on some rough paper the same size as the cushion, cut out the pieces and arrange them to your satisfaction. They can be used as paper patterns when you cut out your material shapes. Tack these in position and appliqué them to the front of the cushion by hand, or machine zig-zag stitch. (Remember to leave the tops of the carriages open!) Join the front to the back with the gusset strip. If you plan to wash the cover frequently, you may want to include a zip-fastener or other easy opening. Otherwise you can just leave one end open, while you stuff in the foam block – working it well into the corners – and then stitch up the final seam.

Restricting the movement of toys

Children with very poor motor control often have difficulty in keeping their toys in one place, or putting them where they want. Even with the help of our faithful friend Velcro attached to toys and to a playboard, the problem may not be solved, for it is difficult to place the furry patch of Velcro tape on the toy squarely onto the rough side on the playboard.

There is a material called Expoloop which overcomes this problem. Expoloop is a looped nylon material made in many colours, which is normally sold as a covering for display boards used in schools or at exhibitions. Self-adhesive tabs are supplied with it, and these can be attached to the backs of pictures, lists, exhibits etc. – in our case, to toys – which can then be put *anywhere* on a board covered with this material. It is this advantage which makes it particularly suitable for use with children who have cerebral palsy and/or a visual handicap. Expoloop can be obtained from Hestair Hope, (*see* p. 188).

A 'Sticky' Playboard

Quick

Romayne Gayton,
Teacher of Visually
   Handicapped Children

Here is a playboard which is designed to be used by multiply handicapped children. It has two play surfaces, both covered with Expoloop, so it is possible for two children to use it at the same time. The playboard itself is shaped like the ridged roof of a house and it is made from three pieces of plywood. Two of these need to be fairly large, say 600 x 450 mm, to form the play surfaces. The third piece makes the base. Its width will determine the tilt of the play surfaces and consequently their stability. If they are too upright and a child presses hard, they are more likely to be knocked over. For the dimensions above, a base measuring 600 x 250 mm is suitable. For anyone without carpentry skills, an easy way to join the three pieces of wood together is to use strong sticky tape. End on, the playboard now makes a tunnel the shape of an isosceles triangle. Using a fabric adhesive, cover the play surfaces with Expoloop. Cut this generously, and tuck the surplus over the edges of the play surfaces, sticking them securely at the back. Lastly, apply the self-adhesive tabs to the chosen toys.

When two children want to use the board at the same time, it can be placed on the table between them. One can play with rattles, strings of cotton reels or feely toys attached to her side. Opposite, her friend may be making a pattern with wooden or foam bricks. (The self-adhesive tabs must be applied to each face of a brick so that whichever way it is presented to the board it will stick to it.)

For toy library use, make a large bag for the board and keep all the toys (fitted with tabs) that go with it in the triangular space between the play surfaces.

If you want a folding board which is easier to store, dispense with the wooden base and drill a hole in each of the bottom corners of the play surfaces. Join them together with two lengths of piping cord poked through the holes and knotted on the outside. The board now opens and closes like a tressel. At playtime, wedge something solid (the ever useful telephone directory?) to act as a spacer between the Expoloop surfaces. This will stop them from closing up or toppling over.

A Flat Expoloop Playboard

Quick

A teacher in a school for children with cerebral palsy used a flat base board covered with this useful material and a set of cutlery with self-adhesive tabs attached, to help her group practise the skill of laying a place at table.

Another advantage of Expoloop is that you can draw on it with a marker pen. For play purposes, the above board could be marked out and used as the background for a roadway layout. Trees and houses could have tabs applied to fix them firmly in place, while the vehicles are left free to move wherever the child decides to push them.

An Easel for a Child Sitting Up in Bed

Long-lasting

Selina Marks,
Hospital Play Specialist

Selina removed the legs from an unwanted double-sided easel – one of those with a hinged top and fitted with folding metal spacer brackets to fix the sloping surfaces rigidly apart. One side of the easel was left as a blackboard and, of course, large sheets of paper for drawing or painting could be clipped to this. Two self-adhesive hooks were stuck to the top of the blackboard. These were used to hang up jumping jacks or goodie bags. The reverse side was covered with self-adhesive cork tiles, and acted as a pin-board for pictures, 'get well' cards etc.

The truncated easel rested on a hospital bed-table which had a high lip round the edge. This kept the easel firmly in place. The short legs of the bed-table fitted comfortably over the short legs of the child in bed! At mealtimes the easel could be folded away and the bed-table used normally.

The requirements for individual children can vary so

17

much that it is up to the person adapting (or making) a table easel to think about size, *stability* and the possible uses such a play surface might have, e.g. a metal surface could be exchanged for cork tiles if toys with magnets or magnetic tape are likely to be used.

Note. Magnets can be bought in various shops – ironmongers, toy shops, in the kitchen-ware department of multiple stores. Magnetic tape is also available in some shops and can always be obtained from E. J. Arnold and Hestair Hope listed among the suppliers on p. 187. Metal surfaces can be found in large toy shops (usually sold complete with magnetic letters and numbers). In the toy library, we used the side panel from an unwanted gas stove with its sharp edges suitably masked. A large biscuit baking tray will also serve the purpose.

Use a Table Top Play Corner

Quick

Judy Denziloe,
Development Worker,
Save the Children Fund

Here is a lovely cheap idea which could solve a very common problem. How can you help a seated child keep his toys conveniently on top of the table when his jerky movements often sweep them to the floor? The answer may be to provide a wedge-shaped cardboard corner which will form a wall round the child's play surface and so help him to keep his toys within reach. All you need is a sizeable square cardboard carton from the super-market. Cut it diagonally in half and use one piece to make the triangular play space. The child's toys can be played with on the bottom of the half box and the two high sides will prevent them from being pushed away. If appropriate, you can make holes in the sides and dangle toys from them.

The table top play corner will probably need stabilis-ing. It can be stuck to the table top with masking tape, wedged in place with something heavy – the telephone directory?, sandbags?, a covered brick? – or if a few judicious holes are made at the bottom of the sides, the whole affair can be securely tied down.

PLANNING A PLAY SESSION

Susan Myatt, a parent, who belongs to the Kingston Toy Library has described the daily play sessions she shares with her little son. Before he was *taught* to play, he would never appear to notice a toy. He would walk on it, bump into it or slide round it, behaving as though it simply wasn't there. Left to his own devices, he would find something to spin or flick between his finger and thumb to the exclusion of any other activity. He would keep this up with great 'concentration' over a long period of time. Now, after many play sessions, he is beginning to come out of his shell. He can enjoy a variety of toys, including tray puzzles which he can do on his own, and simple picture matching games he can play with other people, for he is now willing to wait for his turn. He will look you in the eye, hold hands, enjoy a cuddle now and then, come when he is called, wave 'good-bye' etc. etc! Every school holiday when he visits the toy library, it is lovely to see the progress he is making, largely due to his special playtimes.

To get the full benefit from a play session, the child must have the adult's undivided attention. The toys must be presented and used in a way which imposes a certain amount of discipline on the child, for this helps him to concentrate his attention on the matter in hand.

Now for some practical tips. Susan suggests that before even thinking about toys, you give some thought to planning the environment. Choose a room which is quiet, well lit, warm but not stuffy, and clear of distractions – no television talking to itself in the corner or baby practising its crawling on the floor! Make sure the table you use is a comfortable height for the child. A glossy surface is distracting, and should be avoided if possible. The ideal surface is white matt Fablon. Push the table against a blank wall – not in front of the window, where the view outside could be more entertaining than the toys you offer. The best chair to use is one with a semicircular back that curves round the child and makes it more difficult for him to wriggle off.

For maximum success, the play session should take place at the same time every day, when the child is not hungry or tired and interruptions are not expected. First plan the session in your mind. Don't try to be too ambitious, but give yourself realistic aims. Start with a very short session. Choose an activity your child enjoys and can do with your help. Then introduce something new, for a short while at first. Extend the time in the next session. Always finish off with something you *both* really enjoy – perhaps an active game, singing or clapping, or playing with a soft ball – so that the session ends on a note of happy cooperation and achievement, and in a controlled way. Follow the same routine every day, so that the child learns what is expected of him, but allow for enough variety to prevent you both from becoming bored. (If you live near a toy library, different toys can be borrowed as you need them. For information about toy libraries, *see* p. 192.)

Before you both sit at the table, arrange the toys in the order in which you will offer them, but keep them hidden. This is important. If you have to leave your chair to fetch the next toy, the chances are your child will be up and away too, and the spell will be broken. If the toy has several loose pieces, keep them in a bag and present them one at a time or let the child dip in. This helps to hold his interest, and can prevent him from sweeping them to the floor.

At the end of the session, all the toys you have played with should be put away until next time. This makes them special. If they are left around, the chances are the child will use them for spinning, flicking, etc., and this behaviour could be repeated in the next session. *But* there must always be a box of other toys and bits and pieces that he can play with on his own at any time. Put in things that are texturally interesting or make a noise. An empty egg box or some large buttons on a piece of elastic, or a pebble in a tin could turn out to be the day's winner!

'PLAY HELPS' FOR A CHILD WITH SHORT ARMS

Jenny Buckle, a parent who is a member of the Newton Abbot Toy Library has some suggestions for overcoming this problem. Imagine a busy little toddler in this situation, taking his first unsteady steps with his brand new baby walker, clutching at the handle for support. Unless this has been extended to meet his hands, he is likely to topple onto it, bumping his face and knocking his feet against the base. An uncomfortable situation for the poor child, and one unlikely to increase his confidence! Extend the handle and you have another problem. The balance of the toy is now upset and the front wheels easily leave the ground, leaving the unlucky toddler without the support he relies on. This situation illustrates the need for two considerations. Does the handle of *any* fourwheeled push-along toy need adapting to fit the child? Does the toy need extra weight over the front axle to prevent it from tipping up? Some baby walkers are designed to ensure stability. The rear wheels project behind the child (*see* Educational Suppliers p. 187). If the toddler is using a standard baby walker, where the handle is over the back axle, remove some of the wooden bricks from the tray and replace them with a house brick to weigh down the front wheels. Cover the brick with a piece of material to improve its appearance and make it more pleasant to handle. The padded brick can also be used to add weight to a doll's pram to make it less likely to tip up.

The brick could not be used in one instance where the child's favourite toy was a dog on wheels. The shape of the framework of the toy made it impossible to strap on the brick, so the necessary weight was added by giving the dog a special collar of 'lucky' stones (those with a hole in them) picked up on the beach.

Tools, such as spades and rakes to use in the sand pit (and later on for gardening) will also need their handles extending. With metal tools, the original wooden handle can have a piece spliced on, or a larger handle inserted. With one-piece plastic tools, a longer wooden handle can be tightly bound to the existing one, using string or parcel tape.

Some children need to grip a surface which is fatter than the one supplied. There are several ways of padding out a handle. It can be bandaged with rag, or have sponge foam wrapped round it; it can be built up with a binding of thick wool, or be wrapped round with lots of thick rubber bands. A bicycle handle bar grip may be just what is needed.

For an older child who likes to play with fiddly toys with lots of small pieces (like *Lego* or *Play People*), there is often a problem in preventing the tiny parts from spreading over the table top – and out of reach. Jenny suggests a solution. Confine the pieces within an empty picture frame. The cake turntable (p. 12) can also be useful for holding all the spare bits and pieces.

When it comes to drawing or writing, it is easier to reach the paper if it is clipped to a sloping surface. Pencils may need extending. This can be done by putting two together. Lay them on the table, blunt ends abutting and leads pointing outwards. Bind them together firmly, using plastic tape or wide Sellotape. If the joint is saggy, it can be splinted with a match or cocktail stick. This extended pencil has the added advantage that if the lead in contact with the paper should happen to snap, there is a spare one at the other end! (The child using this elongated pencil will presumably be holding it near the top, so there should be no danger of him poking himself in the face.)

Long-handled paint brushes are available from all good toy shops, or from Educational Suppliers, p. 187.

Part II

CREATING THE TOOLS OF PLAY

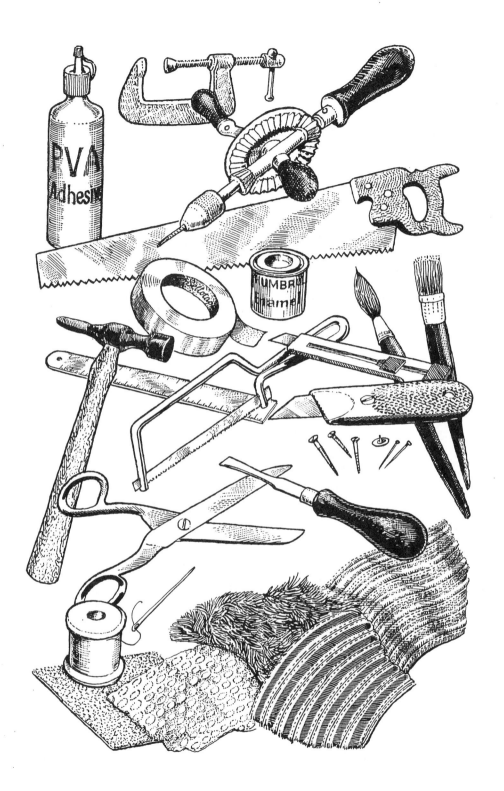

ACTIVITY

Junk Toys to Hang Up for Children to Biff, Grab or Kick

Instant or Quick

At Linden Bennet School one of the teachers hangs up a plastic sweet jar with a few coloured cotton reels inside. When the jar is set swinging the reels rattle together. The jar makes a large target which even children with very poor coordination can manage to hit.

In another part of the room a clown hangs from an elastic loop which emerges from the top of his head. This is made from an old tennis ball covered with material from an unwanted pair of tights and liberally thatched with bright red rug wool 'hair'. The clown reminds me of the Michelin Man made from motor tyres. He is curvacious and cuddly. The Linden Bennet clown is made from a multitude of cloth circles which have all had a running stitch threaded round the edge. Each thread has been drawn up tightly (and securely finished off) to make the cloth into a flat floppy cushion about half the size of the original circle. Some of these are strung together on round elastic to form the arms. Others form the legs and the elastic through their middles continues up through the larger body circles and the tennis ball head to emerge as the hanging loop. The arms are attached to the body by tying them to these central threads (about two circles below the neck). Large jingle bells are stitched to the ends of the arms to represent hands, and smaller ones make the bobbles down his front. For feet, the clown has two large wooden rings — usually used in macramé work, but in this case ideal for the children to pull and so set the bells a-ringing.

Materials
- Circles of cloth: cotton, felt, or any scraps that are brightly coloured and not too thick to gather up. You

will need eight for each arm, and ten for each leg, about the size of a saucer and ten larger ones for the body. Use a tea plate as a template for these.

- A tennis ball.
- Old tights and scraps of felt for the face.
- Wool for hair, or fur fabric, raffia etc.
- Two large bells for the hands; smaller ones for the front of the body.
- Two large rings for the feet; macramé rings, plastic bracelets etc.
- Round hat elastic to string the clown together.

A Trail of Noisy Objects

Instant

Pam Courtney,
Deputy Head Teacher,
St Anne's School

Most children are constantly on the move, exercising both their muscles and their brains as they explore their surroundings and learn by all the new experiences and discoveries that come their way. A child with a visual handicap often needs to be coaxed from the security of his own special corner. The same reluctance to explore can often be a problem with some slow learners who may seem perfectly happy to stay put. If this state of affairs is not discouraged, such children are unlikely to develop either physically or mentally as quickly as they should. One way of persuading reluctant movers 'to have a go' is to follow Pam's suggestion and lay a trail of noisy objects.

Her intention is to lure the child on from one exciting noisemaker to the next, and in the pursuit of this

objective she makes use of *anything* that has child-appeal. The trail could include favourite noisy toys and rattles, the ever popular saucepan (or tin tray) and wooden spoon, or even an unfamiliar junk rattle like a few stones in a tin. At first, the child will have to be introduced to the idea of moving on from one noise-maker to the next. Perhaps he starts by playing happily with a familiar rattle. When this begins to pall, his attention may be attracted by playing a xylophone softly, fairly close to him, but just out of reach. If he wants to know more about the fascinating new sound he hears, he must move towards it, encouraged by your voice, and discover it for himself. At a later stage, when he feels more confident, the trail of noisy objects can be laid in a line across the floor, or round the edge of the carpet for him to discover in his own time. If the child is visually handicapped, this will begin to give him an idea of the layout of the room, and help him to find his way around.

A Large Light Noisy Ball

Easy, but fairly time consuming to make

Mandy Smith,
Parent and Helper,
Greenwich Toy Library

Balls of all sizes can be found in every good toy shop, but there are many children for whom these hold no appeal. A child with a visual handicap needs to *hear* where the ball is going, and for children who are slow learners or have a physical handicap an ordinary ball is sure to *move too quickly.*

Mandy suggests making a custom-built large, light, noisy ball in papier mâché. This uses a technique familiar to most children of Middle School age. If you have young, able-bodied members in your family, the making of this toy is a job that might be delegated to them. The ball is made by covering a sphere with many layers of paper and paste which will dry into a hard shell. This is cut in half and removed from the sphere. Something to make a noise is put between the two halves which are joined together again by yet more layers of paper and paste. The finished ball is painted in bright colours.

Materials
- A sphere large enough to make a suitable mould. This may be damaged when the paper shell is removed, so an old football which has been punctured but still retains its shape would be suitable. Alternatively, a balloon can be used. It is difficult to

27

blow this into a perfectly round shape, but that does not matter – the finished ball may roll more slowly and erratically which might be an advantage!

- Some Vaseline to smear on the mould. This makes it easy to remove the paper shell cleanly. If you use a balloon, it will be destroyed anyway, so you need not worry about a greasy covering.
- Lots of paper torn into small pieces. You can use newspaper, brown paper, even paper torn from the corrugated cardboard used to make grocery cartons.
- PVA adhesive, diluted with a little water (for economy) so that it is the consistency of single cream.
- A noisy filling.
- Paint for the decoration. Emulsion for the undercoat, Humbrol Enamel for the pattern.

Method

Cover the greased mould with several layers of paper, say four if you are using brown paper, more if the paper is thinner. Make sure the scraps of paper are properly stuck down, especially at the edges. It is a good idea to cover the mould completely with one type of paper, then make the next layer with a different one. This way it is easy to see what parts have been covered properly, and the ball will not have thin places. When the paper covering is thick enough and thoroughly dry, remove it from the mould by slicing it in half. Decide on the sort of noise you want the ball to make. You can use a little rice or a few dried peas for a soft sound. Marbles, pebbles or gravel will make more noise. You might use bells (from a pet shop or a vandalised toy) or a mixture of any of these suggestions.

Put your chosen noisemaker in one half of the paper shell. Cover this with the other half and hold the ball together with strips of masking tape. Then cover the join properly with layers of paper and paste. When this has dried, you can give the ball an undercoat of emulsion paint. This covers up the newsprint or dullness of the brown paper and the final colours will be much brighter. The final stage is to 'decorate to taste' as they say in cookery books! Choose very bright colours and a bold design. Remember the advantage of 'high contrast', especially for children with a visual handicap. The best paint for the top coat is Humbrol Enamel.

A Really Huge Game of Draughts

Instant, providing you have a ready supply of washing-up bowls

Hazel Nowell,
Surrey Play Council

This incredible outdoor version of a traditional table top game was played by a group of senior pupils at a Special School for children with mild learning difficulties. The 'draught board' was marked out in chalk on the tarmac surface of the playground, each square having sides of about half a metre. Such enormous squares needed correspondingly large draughts. Washing-up bowls in two distinct colours were used for the purpose. The game could be played by two people in the traditional way. With such a huge 'board' to cover, they certainly had plenty of exercise! If a group of children wanted to play, they would divide into teams, appoint a 'director' for each side and then each player would move a draught bowl as instructed. Players waiting to move could use the bowls as a seat.

This game requires concentration and controlled movement. Played as a 'quietener' after more energetic games, it could appeal to all sorts of older children. Those in wheelchairs could be human draughts.

A smaller version of the game also works well. Forget about washing-up bowls. Substitute the plastic ones normally used for breakfast cereals. Draw smaller squares to fit them. Hazel suggests that for children who can only use one hand, or otherwise have difficulty in moving even these draughts, door knobs can be fitted to the bottoms (now the tops) of the bowls to make them easier to handle.

Giant Building Bricks

Quick, Group or Individual

Marie Madeline Reymond,
Switzerland

Are you searching for something which will encourage children to move, to balance, and to use both hands? Perhaps Marie Madeline has an answer. In the photograph she has sent me the children in her Swiss toy library are demonstrating all these skills as they play with special bricks made from shoeboxes. Top marks to the person who first thought of using these as an oversize construction set! A few boxes stacked up give a spectacular result for comparatively little effort. Given a sufficient quantity, you can even build your own hidey house.

Shoeboxes are usually regarded as 'disposables', so

are cheap and easily obtainable. To convert them into building bricks, it is sensible to stuff them (to give them extra strength), tape on the lids, and for cosmetic purposes to cover them. The stuffing can be just scrunched up newspaper. At this point, it is possible to adjust the *weight* of each box (a feature which may appeal to therapists and make the bricks especially suitable for a particular child). For a light box, polystyrene chips can be used. For more weight, hide a few stones among the crumpled newspaper, and for a really heavy weight use a therapy sandbag. To prevent the contents of the boxes from spilling out, secure the lids firmly with plastic parcel tape. Cover the outsides of the boxes to add to their attractiveness and strength. You could use cheap coloured 'sugar' paper, normally used for children to paint on, or pieces of wrapping paper stuck on patchwork fashion. The ends of rolls of washable wallpaper could be ideal if the children are inclined to dribble. If the bricks are likely to be heavily used, it might be worthwhile to cover them with fabric. The shoeboxes appear again on p. 71 as giant tactile dominoes.

Materials
- A quantity of identical shoeboxes – as many as you can conveniently store!
- Stuffing, for extra strength, i.e. polystyrene chips, newspaper with perhaps a stone added; sandbag.
- Plastic parcel tape for securing down the lids.
- Decorative outer cover in paper or cloth.

Build a Town

Quick

R. L.

Do you ever organise a toy library festivity where you are fortunate enough to have that rare luxury, plenty of space? If so, the following tale may interest you – and the children.

Every year, at the hospital for the mentally handicapped where I was working, we would have one glorious day, known as 'Fun Day', when the entire population of the hospital would visit the playing field, take part in all sorts of activities, and share a vast picnic. In the central arena, there would be a succession of events like a fancy dress parade, or a marching band, or a display of dancing. All round the edge of the field were the 'side shows'. Here the residents could enjoy a stick of candy floss, fish for plastic ducks in a tub of water, try their luck with the hoop-la and lucky dip or thoroughly enjoy themselves hurling sponges at a charge nurse with his head poking through an Aunt Sally board!

My contribution to the jollification was to provide a huge quantity of cardboard boxes of all shapes and sizes which were transformed into giant building bricks. Residents who attended the Adult Training Centre had stuck the flaps down with sticky tape, and then painted the boxes with 'left overs' of emulsion paint that nobody

wanted. The result of all this industry was a large heap of multicoloured cubes just waiting for someone to build them into something! As it happened, the first resident to visit my corner of the field was a very tall man. He spent a happy five minutes building a high tower of single bricks piled on top of each other. Luckily he realised the largest should go at the bottom, so managed to achieve a monumental edifice, taller even than himself. It was visible from some distance away, and soon attracted other would-be builders. Throughout the afternoon, walls, tower blocks, enclosures and 'ruins' were made. All this involved a great deal of thought, bending and stretching, balancing, using both

31

hands etc., but above all, judging by the reactions of both builders and spectators, it helped to put the fun in 'Fun Day'!

Strong and Chunky Stilts

Long-lasting

Noah's Ark Toy Library,
Melbourne,
Australia

Stilt walkers were an attraction at mediaeval fairs, and still are at many modern circuses. Generations of children have spent happy hours learning to 'walk tall' on stilts made from square poles with blocks of wood screwed on for footrests and the tops rounded off to make handles. Younger children like to try walking on a pair of tins. Two holes are punched through the sides and pieces of string threaded through so that the tins can be lifted alternately with each step. Tins have become thinner over the years and are likely to crumple under the weight of an older child. Not so these stilts from Australia!

They are made from cube-shaped blocks of wood which can be cut to fit any size of child just by making them slightly larger than the width of his foot. Each block has a hole drilled through it to take the rope handle. When the child is standing up, roughly measure the distance from his hand to the floor. Cut two pieces of rope, thick string or thick piping cord, twice this length, with a little bit extra 'for luck'! Thread the cord through each block and knot the ends together. (If you want to make a neat job, put a dab of glue on the knots and hide them inside the holes.) Both blocks are now dangling from a large loop of cord. The child puts a foot on each, holds a loop in each hand and tries to walk. First the hand and foot on one side must be lifted and moved, then the other. This requires concentration, coordination and lots of practice. Luckily the stilts are so near the ground that toppling off is fun, and not hazardous. As skill increases, the child can try walking sideways or backwards, or climbing a shallow step.

See also
Polystyrene Plane, p. 160
Another Target Game, p. 162
Two Sock Games for Letting Off Steam, p. 163

BLOWING

BODY AWARENESS

BUTTONS AND BOWS

BLOWING

'I'll huff and I'll puff and I'll *blow* your house in', says the Big Bad Wolf in the story of the three little pigs. Young children love the predictability of the punch line and always happily 'huff and puff' as the story demands. For those of us who can manage it, it is easy to take this simple action for granted. Not everyone is so lucky. Some children have to learn special breathing techniques because of their physical disabilities. Others must be taught to control their breath, so that they can make the sounds of speech. Apart from therapeutic reasons, being able to blow can be great fun! Babies discover this when they object to the taste of their cereal and splatter it everywhere and, of course, blowing bubbles and games like Blow Football depend upon it.

Sometimes children must be coaxed to blow. They need to be shown a simple activity where the result of their 'huffing and puffing' is immediately obvious. Some time-worn ways of doing this are by:

- draping a length of toilet paper over the child's head for him to blow away;
- blowing at a candle flame to make it deflect (where it is *safe* to do so);
- blowing at a downy feather (from a pillow) to make it float in the air;
- blowing at a small piece of crumpled tissue paper. (If it is flat, it is more difficult to get airborne, and tends to stick to the table);
- blowing a ping-pong ball over the edge of a table.

Once a child has learnt to control his breath, he can use the skill in many ways, and revel in his achievements. He can:

- blow out his birthday candles;
- blow the seeds of a dandelion 'clock' to tell the time;
- blow his sailing boat across the bath;
- with a straw, blow watery paint over the surface of a sheet of shiny paper to make a pattern;
- blow a plastic windmill to make it turn;
- blow a mouth organ (buy a good quality one with no rough edges);
- on a cold day 'herr' on the window pane and make pictures in the steam;
- blow up a paper bag – and pop it to scare everyone;
- make an ear-splitting shriek by blowing across the edge of a blade of grass held tightly across the gap made by pressing his thumbs together. (I taught this trick to a toy library member with a hearing loss. He was delighted, but I am not so sure about his mother!)
- and, of course, indulge in one of the joys of childhood . . .

Blowing bubbles

For some children, it may well be necessary to prepare the way. When first presented with a straw in his mouth, the child may think he is being offered a pleasant drink and will probably suck instead of blow. The resulting mouthful of soapy water could be such a shock that he is put off the idea for ever! One way of making sure this does not happen is to use a transparent drinking straw, or better still, a length of narrow polythene tubing normally used in brewing home-made wine. This can quickly be removed from the child's mouth if the liquid is seen to travel upwards. This same tubing, if long enough, can make bubble blowing possible for children who cannot sit up. Providing they have sufficient lung power, they can use it to raise their pile of bubbles from quite a distance.

Once having learnt to bubble efficiently, the obvious place for all this frothy activity is in the bath. At other times, a lot of mess can be avoided by putting the bowl of bubble mixture inside a larger bowl, or on a tray covered with a towel. This way the bubbles can pile up and spill over the edge of their container, but the child and his surroundings should remain dry.

If you want a change from ordinary bubble blowing, try these suggestions.

1. A teacher at the Sense Centre (for Deaf/Blind Children) puts the bubble mixture in an unusual container – such as a teapot. Try it!
2. The Nursery Class at Bedelsford School use their bubbles to make patterns. A small amount of powder paint is added to the bubble mixture. This is put in a pudding basin. When an impressive mound of bubbles has been raised, a sheet of paper is pressed gently on the surface. Some bubbles will stick to this. It is lifted off carefully and put aside to dry. The bubbles gradually pop, leaving a delicate pattern of overlapping coloured circles.
3. Sometimes, at bath time, a Care Assistant at a children's home finds time to make the children special gloves – or shoes, or vests, or knee pads – by covering the selected parts of their bodies with a thick layer of bubbles. These feel warm and comfortable, and tickle as they pop.
4. The Occupational Therapists at the Manor Hospital suggest blowing bubbles the old-fashioned way. You need a bowl of water, a bar of soap and a tube to blow down. The cardboard interior of a toilet roll or a newspaper rolled into a tube and kept in shape with wool or Sellotape will do. Dip the end of the tube into the water and rub it across the bar of soap. This may have to be done several times before a soap film forms across the mouth of the tube. When it does, blow gently down the tube to form a huge bubble. With practice, enormous ones can be blown, and if the tube is given a certain little flick, the bubbles can be made to fly away (I am reliably informed!)

Ideas contributed by Pam Courtney, Christine Cousins, Lorraine Crawford and R.L.

Puff Ball

Quick

Jusuf Raymond,
Student,
Handicap Education and Aids
    Research Unit (HEARU),
City of London Polytechnic

There is a cheap, but fragile, toy on the market which is used by many Speech Therapists because it is an excellent device for encouraging a child to blow. The toy consists of a small pipe – like a pipe for smoking tobacco – and a small light plastic ball which rests in the bowl of the pipe. When the child blows slowly and steadily, this can be made to rise on the column of air and stay suspended above the pipe. This takes considerable skill and breath control. To start with, what usually happens is that the child gives a hearty puff and the ball shoots across the room, causing great hilarity as the unfortunate fielder tries to catch it!

Jusuf has made a strong version of this toy. It works very well and can be used by children who cannot manage the one above. Jusuf's model is made from a small plastic funnel, about 9 cm in diameter, and a length of narrow polythene tubing of the right size to fit snugly inside the stem. Both these items are available from a shop that sells equipment for home wine brewing, (e.g. large branches of Boots). The advantage of using these materials is that the funnel can be some distance from the child's face and he can see it easily without squinting. *Anything* can be put in the funnel for him to blow out, starting perhaps with a little bit of teased-out cotton wool fluff or a tiny feather, and gradually increasing the weight of the blown object as his skill improves. The child using Jusuf's toy was able to blow out a ping-pong ball, and was delighted when his baby brother was sent scuttling after it to act as ball boy.

Method
Push the end of the tubing through the stem of the funnel so that it protrudes into the bowl. Wrap masking tape around the end of the tube, leaving the last 20 mm uncovered. Give a little downward tug and you will find the masking tape acts as a plug to hold the tube firmly in place in the neck of the funnel.

If you find your pipe does not work as efficiently as you feel it should, take another tip from Jusuf and punch three holes in the uncovered end of the tubing. I can't explain why this slight change in the air flow should help to lift the object in the funnel, but it does! No doubt a question of aerodynamics.

BODY AWARENESS

Children who suffer from brain damage can have great difficulty in controlling parts of their bodies and may not even be aware of the position of their hands and feet. Parents, teachers and therapists work hard to help the children to be more conscious of the various areas of their bodies – the first step in encouraging movement and control. The following ideas have all been used so successfully with certain children that some of them have almost become traditional. Among them may be something that could help a child you know.

- Christine Cousins (Educational Psychologist) covers a plastic washing-up liquid bottle with a textured material to give it a pleasant feel, and hands it to a child for her to puff air on herself. Put a few drops of the child's favourite perfume in the bottle to make this activity even more desirable.
- Samantha Neal (Teacher, Dysart School) uses a large cardboard carton, such as those used in packaging a fridge or washing machine. She lines it with mirror tiles and sits the child inside, so that any movement she makes will be reflected back to her.
- Samantha also uses a hoop with balloons tied all around it. The hoop is suspended encircling the child, so that when he moves his arms, he sets all the balloons in motion (*see* Mobiles, p. 116).
- Lena Baum (Specialist in Play) makes a tickling brush from a strip of paper. Fold the paper in half lengthways, and with scissors snip a fringe from one edge to the centre. Roll up the paper tightly so that the uncut half makes the handle and the fringed paper the 'bristles'. Hold the roll together with a rubber band or Sellotape.
- For a softer tickle, use a make-up brush, a shaving brush, a feather duster or a lambswool back sponge. For a rough rub, go to the Body Shop and see if they have what you want among their range of massage aids. They also have a wide choice of massage oils. If you want pure oils without additives (for children with allergies) search in the Health Food Shops or Boots.

- Mrs Ross (a Toy Library parent) makes wrist or ankle rattles for hand and foot awareness. All you need to make one is a small round flat tin. Put something inside to make the rattle, decorate it and attach it to a strap. The strap should fit comfortably, but not tightly. Velcro is useful for joining the ends together. A sweat band would also be suitable.

- Christine Cousins reminds us that a balloon loosely attached by a string to a wrist or ankle will also help a child to realise when she has moved that particular part of her body.

- Teachers at the Sense Centre (for Deaf/Blind Children, some with additional handicaps) say some children like to have a small strip of masking tape stuck to their legs, fingers etc. for them to pull off. It can be removed quite easily (unlike sticking plaster!) and gives a pleasant sensation.

- They also suggest encouraging a child to play with popcorn which sticks to the fingers and can then be sucked off. This delightful activity *must* be supervised to avoid any possible danger of choking.

- Draw a face on the palm or back of the child's hand.

- Use finger puppets and put them on the child's hand. For children who cannot uncurl their fingers (to wear a finger puppet) try a sock or mitt puppet. To make one of these, just decorate the sock (or mitt!) with button eyes and a few strands of wool hair – perhaps with a brightly coloured bow of ribbon on the top. Place it over the child's hand for her to wave about and join in the fun. An oven glove makes a good puppet for a large hand.

- For children who can make their thumb and middle finger touch each other, and therefore are able to operate a glove puppet, try sewing metal buttons to the hands (or paws) of a glove puppet. Play some rousing music on the tape recorder, and the child can join in by making her puppet clap its hands together as though it is playing the cymbals.

- Put thimbles on the child's fingers and help her to rub a ridgy surface, like the washboards in the days of skiffle! Some doorstep protectors are made in grooved metal and can be bought at builders' merchants. Fluted cardboard will not last as long, but it gives the same pleasant sensation when it is rubbed.

Head, Body and Legs Card

Quick

Chemène Hoare,
Student,
Toy Making Course,
London College of Furniture

With a little jiggery pokery and a sheet of card, you can make a character with interchangeable heads, bodies and legs. The more incongruous the result, the funnier the children will find it! Try out the idea first on a sheet of notepaper. You may want to alter the proportions in your final version.

Mark out your card (or paper) into three equal columns. Fold in the side columns to cover the central one. Open the paper out. Draw a person – head, body and legs – to fill the middle section. With horizontal cuts, divide each side piece into three flaps which will correspond to the head, body and legs of the central figure. (The head flap will be smaller than the others.) Fold in the top flap on the left hand side so that it covers the central head. On it draw a new head, making sure it lines up with the central body. Fold in the left hand middle flap and draw another body to line up with the head and the original legs. Finish off the new person by folding in the bottom flap and drawing a pair of legs. Repeat the process with the three right hand flaps. You should now have a central figure with interchangeable parts.

Bear in mind the interests of the child you are aiming to entertain and draw the figures accordingly. Let your imagination wander too far and you might end up with a ballet dancer wearing a bowler hat and football boots!

This idea turns up again on p. 46. In this version the clothes of the central figure can be colour coordinated.

See also
Hand-prints, p. 86
Circular Mobiles a Child Can Sit Inside, p. 119
Egbert, the Egg Box King, p. 137

BUTTONS AND BOWS

It is a fact of life that children's clothes often need to be put on in a hurry. A kindly adult frequently rescues the half-clad child, whipping through his buttons and zips without giving him the chance to do it himself because the school coach must not be kept waiting. There is a moral here which one teacher in a special school has recognised. She allows plenty of time at the end of the afternoon session for everyone to try hard to put on their going-home clothes with as little assistance as possible, and she arranges for some children to help each other by finishing off zips started by an adult.

Undoubtedly, all children need practice in manipulating buttons and zips or tying laces, and most schools have their own collection of devices to help the pupils increase their skills (e.g. Montessori button or laces frames). These are all useful, but few can claim to be *fun*! Children will work on them because they are instructed to, but if the pill of learning can have a modest coating of sugar, the children will swallow it more willingly and may be motivated to spend a long time trying to improve their skills. Here are some suggestions for applying the sugar coating.

For people who do not enjoy sewing

Dressing Dolls

Instant

Provide the children with a few large dolls to dress, preferably rag ones with arms and legs that are easier to bend, and raid the next jumble sale for a collection of clothes – all with their buttons on! – to fit the dolls.

Australian Cushion

Quick

Take a tip from the Handbook of the Association of Australian Toy Libraries and make a useful doodle cushion covered with all sorts of fastenings. Remove the zips from a pair of old trousers; buttons and button-holes from the front of a discarded dress; lacing holes from a worn-out canvas shoe; find an old belt with a buckle on it; and stitch them all firmly to a washable cover which can be put on a cushion. This can rest on the table or child's knee, and will make all the fastenings easier to reach. The Handbook suggests that alternatively, the fastenings can be fixed to a board. The children will react favourably to this trainer, because it contains a *variety* of fastenings from *real* clothes. Maybe they will recognise the fancy buttons from the front of Auntie Maggie's blouse!

For people who enjoy sewing

Button Pictures

Quick

Monica Taylor,
Toy Librarian,
The Rix Toy Library,
Normansfield

A button picture is one in which an essential part is made as a separate piece and must be buttoned on to complete the picture. Monica has made several which can be played with on the table or floor, or hung on the wall. She has found these particularly useful with a little group of children with Down's Syndrome, but they are so colourful and attractive that everyone wants to have a go. They are cut from felt which is easy to use because it does not fray. A backing of iron-on Vilene gives it extra strength and stiffness.

Monica's simplest designs are flowers which are buttoned onto their stalks. (For people of my generation they are reminiscent of Little Weed in 'The Flower Pot Men'.) Slightly more complicated are her button faces. Here two layers in the shape of a face are attached to each other by a few stitches at the top. Buttons are sewn to the bottom piece, and positioned so that, when they are threaded through the appropriate holes in the top piece, they make the eyes, nose and mouth of the face. This can represent an animal or a human.

Two attractive wall hangings decorate the toy library. One shows a circus scene. Undo a zip in a red circle of felt and you reveal a dog jumping through a hoop; a seal juggles with a succession of balls that must be buttoned on; lift the ring master's hat to find the rabbit hiding inside. The other wall hanging represents a country scene. Apples and birds can be buttoned onto the tree,

41

flowers can be attached to the border and there are butterflies and rabbits to be put where the child wishes.

An Unusual Device for Practising Self-Help Skills

Quick

Jonathan Shaw,
Nurse,
The Maudsley Hospital

Imagine a pair of double doors, in this case made of cloth and closed together with buttons and buttonholes. Open these doors to reveal another set that close with press studs. Open these and you are faced with yet a third set, this time tied together with bows. Now you are getting warm! Open these and you will find a final pair closed with a zip-fastener. Undo this to reveal a small pocket with a surprise inside – a sweet? a tiny toy? a picture? – the choice will be up to you, if you decide to make this device.

It is best to begin with the final pocket and sew this to the backing material. Cut this with plenty to spare, for eventually all the doors need to be attached to it. My sewing machine objects to stitching through too many thicknesses of material but, by allowing a wide margin, each pair of doors can be attached outside the previous pair. The device is easier for the children to use if the backing is stiffened. You can either use pelmet stiffening or heavy duty iron-on Vilene, or make the backing in double material and slide a piece of cardboard between the layers. (If you are likely to need to wash the device, this will have to be removed of course.) Making the doors is not difficult, if you tackle the joining edges first, dealing with the way to close them and then hingeing them to the backing piece.

Popper Dollies

Quick

R.L.

These little people are made from two layers of felt with pelmet stiffener sandwiched in between. Their arms are attached to their bodies with press studs, and there is half a stud stitched to the back of one hand with the opposite half sewn to the other. Using this arrangement, all the little people can be linked together to hold hands in a circle or row.

The colours chosen represent the colours of the rainbow (red, orange, yellow, green, blue, purple,) plus black and white. The dolls can have their arms arranged in different positions or even interchanged so that the yellow doll has red sleeves. If you have the stomach for it, remove all the arms. Then jumble them up for the

children to return to their rightful owners by matching the colours.

All this is excellent practice in pushing together the two parts of a press stud – a skill many children find very difficult.

A Bag Full of Surprises

Long-lasting

Mrs Mackee,
Physiotherapist working with
  young visually
  handicapped children

In the course of her work, Mrs Mackee pays many home visits. As part of her stock in trade, she had made herself a large tote bag in brightly coloured sail cloth. The bag is circular and has a firm base, (thick cardboard covered with material, but removable when the bag needs washing). The sides of the bag, both inside and out, have many patch pockets of different shapes and sizes in which various toys can be hidden. Each pocket closes in a different way. Some are easy to open when the Velcro fastening is pulled apart. Others have short zip-fasteners, with pull tags attached to each end, and the more difficult ones have buttons of assorted sizes, and laces which tie in a bow. This arrangement makes the bag very attractive to the children. The fun is not only in opening all the pockets to find the surprises inside but, at the end of playtime, they seem to find it equally diverting to put the toys away again and secure them in their pockets for the next child to find.

A Look and Play Picture Book

Long-lasting

Rosmarie Thomi-Fischli,
Basle,
Switzerland

Rosmarie is a lady who is obviously good at sewing, judging by the photographs she has sent me of the beautiful picture book she has designed. Each page is a collage of simple shapes cut from oddments of various brightly coloured materials and appliquéd to a denim background to form a very effective picture. What makes this book different from an ordinary rag book is the three dimensional touch aided by the detachable bits and pieces forming part of each picture.

On one page (a garden scene) a tree is laden with rosy apples which can be picked by undoing press studs. A row of washing is attached to the line with real miniature plastic pegs. A basket stands on the grass ready to receive the washing – or the apples? Further on in the book, a lady is minding a market stall well stocked with fruit and vegetables attached with Velcro. These can be taken to the kitchen page and 'cooked' in the little pockets shaped like pots and pans that stand on the stove, then served up on the plates hooked to the dresser. One of my favourite pages is the nursery scene. Here the baby can be put in its cot and the curtains over the window drawn together. More delightful pages follow, but one near the end will appeal to a child with a gruesome sense of humour: a fierce alligator swims in the river; small fish and a duck rest in pockets in the water. Undo the zip in the alligator's mouth and he can be made to gobble them up!

Each page in the book measures about 300 mm square. The pictures are arranged back to back. Bias binding neatens three sides while the fourth sides are stitched together to make the spine. The book has two practical touches: the last page has a knapsack, sewn onto the background, which can be unbuckled to store any small leftover pieces; and on the front cover are two buttons which have been worked into the design. These are stitched, top and bottom, near to the right hand edge. Two loops are attached to corresponding places on the back cover and can be hooked over the buttons to keep the pages closed and all the small pieces safe inside.

See also
Dress the Twins, p. 45
Shake and Make, p. 47
Getting it Wrong Again!, p. 154

COLOUR

Coloured Picture Windows

Quick

Angela Smith
Teacher,
Special Care Unit,
Walton Leigh School

Angela cuts two large oblongs in stiff cardboard, and removes the middles so that she ends up with two shapes like a picture frame. She sandwiches coloured cellophane between them to make a window, and repeats the process with other colours. She hangs two or three from a string which stretches across the window. The children like to look through them to see the outside world in a different light (rose tinted glasses?) and on a sunny day the 'windows' make bright patches of colour on the floor. Sometimes a child in a wheelchair is positioned so that the light shines on her hands.

What Colour? Which Box?

Quick

R.L.

I wish I had met Mr Murphy and his Boxes (p. 149) in the days when I was busily trying to think up new and interesting ways of helping children to identify colours. How easy to adapt his idea for this particular purpose by making a collection of shoeboxes, painting them different colours and filling each with objects to match. At first the children could examine all the objects in one box, naming them as they picked them up. (A blue glove, a blue button, a blue car etc.) Another time two boxes could be used together, the contents muddled up and then returned to their rightful places . . . and so on.

Dress the Twins

Quick

Catherine O'Neil,
Speech Therapist

Catherine plays colour matching games using two teddy bears. The idea is to dress the teddies alike. At the simplest level, they can wear necklaces of identical colours, either made from beads, or threaded by the children using coloured drinking straws chopped into small lengths, and pipe cleaners or shoelaces for threaders. The teddies can also be dressed in matching clothes.

45

Fashion Coordinates

Quick

A square of felt with a hole cut in the centre will pass for a poncho, and a bobble hat or scarf can be knitted to match. For children with nimble fingers more sophisticated clothes can be made that are more difficult to put on, and may require fastenings to be closed with Velcro, buttons etc. Obviously, several sets of clothes are required so that the child must make a choice.

For a quick colour matching activity for one child, try adapting Chemène Hoare's 'Head, Body and Legs' card. This time the three figures could wear different outfits which can be made to 'coordinate' by correctly arranging the flaps. (For instructions on how to make it, *see* p. 39.)

The central figure might wear, say, a red hat, yellow jersey and blue skirt (or trousers!) The figure on the tabs on the left could have a yellow hat, blue jersey and red bottom half, while the person on the right hand tabs wears blue on top, red in the middle and yellow at the bottom. Puzzle – fold the card this way and that until the clothes on each person are entirely of one colour.

A Six Colour Card Game

Quick

Joan Thorpe,
Librarian,
Merry-go round Toy Library,
Frimley

Joan has invented a colour recognition game which, in its simplest form, can be made in a matter of minutes. In this case the backs of old Christmas cards are used, and the game will last long enough to be played with a few times. If more care is spent on its creation and the finished cards are protected with sticky-backed plastic, the game will be a durable and interesting one which will be helpful either to young children learning their colours, or to older ones who need to practise colour matching.

The game consists of a pack of cards, each having on it a picture in one of six colours corresponding to the spots on a colour dice. When the dice is rolled, the player can discard a picture of the same colour as that thrown. If the colour on the dice does not match a card in his hand, he can either 'pass', or keep on throwing until he is lucky. The second option finishes the game more quickly! It also gives more individual practice in colour matching, for the child must constantly compare the cards in his hand with the colour on the dice.

To make the game, you need plenty of small cards –

say twenty-four for four players. You also need a colour dice, and six felt pens to match the spots on the dice. These are usually red, blue, green, yellow, black and white. (If you are stumped for a dice, ask at the toy library. Most have a little box full of spares.) Next make a list of things which are familiar to the children and are easy to draw. (You can always trace, or use a stencil or template!) The list might include a tree, house, hat, gloves, socks, saucepan, mug, car, flower etc. Choose six items from your list and draw each say four times, making each copy of the same thing a *different* colour. You don't have to use all the colours for every object. You might end up with a set of cars in white, blue, red and yellow – but no blue tree!

Note. Unprinted playing cards are excellent for making games like this. They are obtainable from Hestair Hope, p. 188.

Shake and Make

Long-lasting

Jackie Mills,
Hospital Play Specialist

This unusual colour matching game is top favourite with the children of Jackie's ward, and it could be equally successful as a family game or with school or residential groups of mixed ability. All can take part on equal terms and there need be no winners or losers. It is also a delightfully different way of practising the skills of colour matching, counting up to six, and doing up press studs. For less able groups, the variety of colours and numbers could be reduced, and Velcro substituted for press studs.

The game consists of a large number of little felt cushions which can be joined together with press studs. There must be six colours (to correspond to the six sides of a dice). Jackie chose red, blue, green, yellow, orange and black. The game also needs two dice, one with black spots from one to six, and the other with a single coloured spot on each face, corresponding to the colours of the cushions. Each child takes his turn at throwing both dice, and then collects cushions as directed. Supposing the dice show three spots and the colour red. The player helps himself to three red cushions, and joins them together with the press studs. Next turn, he might add two blue, then four green etc. until all the cushions are used up.

Forget about the dice, and use the little cushions as a colour matching activity. They can be joined together in

47

a string of all one colour or a sequence of colours can be repeated to make a pattern or a necklace. The children in the hospital ward discovered another possibility. A row of cushions could be propelled down the long ward corridor in a most satisfactory way!

Materials
- Felt in six different colours.
- Kapok or terylene stuffing.
- Press studs (or Velcro).
- Two small foam cubes (about 60 mm) and white material for the cover. Or you can use plastic dice from a game you already have. Blank dice that you can mark yourself are available from Hestair Hope etc., p. 188. (Useful if your group can't yet count up to six!).
- A container for all the pieces. A large transparent plastic jar is ideal.

Method
To make a satisfactory game for four players you need *at least* ten cushions (twenty circles) of each colour. Cut the circles about 50 mm in diameter. Use the foot of the stem of a wine glass or the base of a bottle as a template. Take two circles of one colour and tack them together, leaving a small gap for inserting the stuffing. Fill the cushion with a small ball of stuffing, about the size of a ping-pong ball, and close up the gap. Sew neatly all round the edge. Use the zig-zag stitch on the machine, or blanket stitch, or oversew by hand. Sew one half of a press stud to each side of the cushion, or if you are making for a group who will be unable to manipulate these, use Velcro spots instead.

If you are making your own dice, cover the cubes of foam with white material. On one, sew or stick on spots of coloured felt to match the cushions, and make the other like an ordinary dice by attaching black spots from one to six. (The opposite sides should always add up to seven.)

See also
Popper Dollies, p. 42
Feely Gloves, p. 69
Glove Shops, p. 69
Popper Balls, p. 90
The Disco Window, p. 116
A Good Colour Game for Journeys, p. 126

DOLLS

DOODLE TOYS

Instant Doll

Loet Vos,
Museum of
Childhood,
Toronto

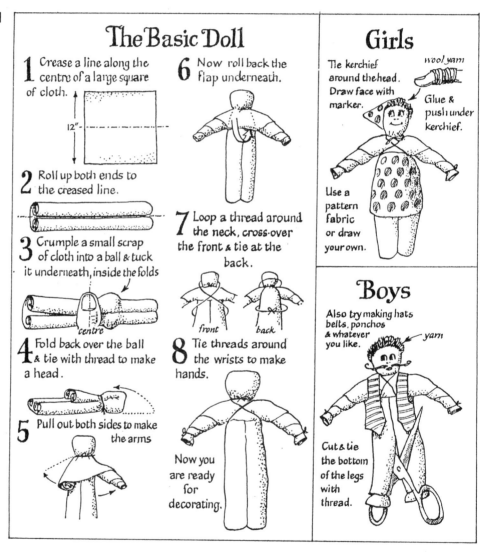

The Basic Doll

1 Crease a line along the centre of a large square of cloth.

12"

2 Roll up both ends to the creased line.

3 Crumple a small scrap of cloth into a ball & tuck it underneath, inside the folds

centre

4 Fold back over the ball & tie with thread to make a head.

5 Pull out both sides to make the arms

6 Now roll back the flap underneath.

7 Loop a thread around the neck, cross-over the front & tie at the back.

front   back

8 Tie threads around the wrists to make hands.

Now you are ready for decorating.

Girls

Tie kerchief around the head. Draw face with marker.

wool yarn

Glue & push under kerchief.

Use a pattern fabric or draw your own.

Boys

Also try making hats belts, ponchos & whatever you like.

yarn

Cut & tie the bottom of the legs with thread.

50

Footnote to Loet Vos' Basic Doll

When James Holmes was a student attending the Toy Making Course at the London College of Furniture, he discovered that if he wrapped pipe cleaners in the rolls of cloth that become the arms and legs of the doll, he could create a figure capable of action! The arms could be bent in different positions, and the legs made to sit or kneel. If the arms were made as long as the legs, the doll could be placed on all fours and turned into an animal.

A Paper Doll

Instant

Lena Baum,
Specialist in Play

Here is how to make another ephemeral doll, this time using two sheets of paper (notepaper, or pages from an exercise book). You also need a rubber band, Sellotape or wool to hold the finished doll together.

Roll one sheet of paper, lengthwise, into a tube. Flatten it, and fold it in half. This will make the head and body. Take *half* the other sheet, and roll it, widthwise, into another tube. Flatten it and put it inside the first piece in the correct position to represent the arms. Fix these in position (rubber band etc.) and mark in the features.

This instant doll is softer and more curvaceous if paper tissues are used. Two rubber bands are needed to make the neck and waist. Draw in the face and hair. This idea might be worth remembering next time you need to amuse a child on a long journey or while waiting for a hospital appointment.

Peg Doll

Quick

Pam Rigley,
Toy Librarian,
Reading

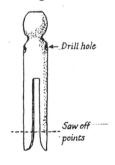
Drill hole

Saw off points

This doll is made from an old-fashioned dolly peg. These are still available if you search around the ironmongers, street markets or handicraft shops.

First saw off the bottoms of the peg, as shown in the picture. Cut higher up if the character you are making is young. Drill a small hole through the body, just below the neck. Thread a pipe cleaner through the hole, glue it in place and bend back the ends to make the hands. Rub the bottoms of the legs with sandpaper, and glue on some pieces of pipe cleaner to make the feet. Paint the head with primer. When this is dry, paint the face, or use felt pens. Make the hair with fur fabric, wool or shredded cloth, and clothe your doll appropriately.

Materials
• A dolly peg

51

- Two pipe cleaners, one for the arms, the other for the feet
- Paint and felt pens
- Scraps of cloth for the clothes

Pipe Cleaner Doll

Quick

Pam Rigley,
Toy Librarian,
Reading

This doll is made from two pipe cleaners. The centre of one is bent around your finger to make a circle for the head. The ends are bent outwards to make the arms, and the tips bent over to form the hands. The other pipe cleaner is threaded through the head circle, twisted together to make the body, then separated for the legs. The ends are bent over to form the feet. Roll a paper hankie into a ball and glue it into the circle to make the face. The doll can be wrapped round with pink wool, or bandaged with strips of paper hankie and paste. Paint the face and hair, and make her some clothes. Her limbs bend beautifully, so she might become a ballerina. All she needs is a circle of net, or even another paper hankie, gathered around her waist to make her a tu-tu.

Materials
- Two pipe cleaners
- A paper hankie or two
- Felt pens or paint for the face
- Scraps of material
- Glue

Straw Dancing Dolly

Quick

Pam Rigley,
Toy Librarian,
Reading

This energetic little doll is made from plastic drinking straws, a cotton wool ball for the head and four beads for the hands and feet. All these are joined together with button thread. First, cut the drinking straw the right size to represent the arms, body and legs. Cut a long piece of thread and begin threading at the neck. Pass the thread down the body and one leg, through a bead (for the foot), back up the leg, down the other leg, through the other foot and back up the leg and body. Hopefully, you now have two ends of thread emerging from the top of the body. Take one end down an arm, through a hand and back up the arm. Join on the other arm with the remaining length of thread at the top of the body and knot both arm threads together before passing them through the head. Finish off by passing one end through a piece of straw and knotting both ends together. Hold the doll by this handle and dangle her about. The weight of the beads for her hands and feet will make her dance with gay abandon!

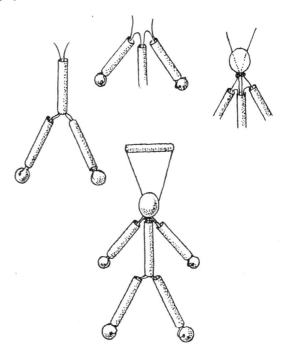

Materials
- Plastic drinking straws
- A cotton wool ball
- Button thread
- Four beads

La Poupée Blanche et Noir

Quick

Mme Schneider,
Teacher of Visually
 Handicapped Children,
Switzerland

Mme Schneider, who works with young visually handicapped children, finds that making toys in black and white can be helpful for those with partial sight. The high contrast in colour makes the toys easier to see, and therefore easier to find, because they stand out from all the surrounding colours in the room.

She makes a delightful little cuddly doll from white material. The features are embroidered in black, the hair is made from black wool, and the clothes are also in black and white. The doll is stuffed with acrylic fibre so it is easily washed.

I made a little dolly in black and white for one of the toy library children, to see if she would like the idea. Mme Schneider has set a trend among our children. Everyone wants one now! Not having any suitable scraps of white material handy, I made my doll from a long white sock. I cut the leg from the foot, and imagined it as the head, body and legs. I slit it up a little way to make the legs, and sewed twice round the raw edges to make strong seams. I stuffed the doll's legs, and stitched across the tops (a) to keep the stuffing in, and (b) to help the finished doll to sit down! I then stuffed the body and tied the sock with several strands of cotton in the best place for the neck. Before stuffing the head, I ran a row of gathering stitches round the top. Once the stuffing was in place, these could be drawn up to close the top of the head. The arms were made from the remaining material in the foot of the sock and sewn in place very firmly.

See also
Families of Feely Dolls, p. 70

DOODLE TOYS

All over the world there are children who love to fiddle with things — in other words, to *doodle*. At this level of play, it can sometimes be hard to provide older children with a variety of fresh experiences. They have seen it all before. That is the problem. Now for some solutions.

A Doodle Ring

Quick

Romayne Gayton,
Teacher of Visually
　　Handicapped Children

Romayne uses a length of clear polythene tubing, and she fuses the ends together to make a fairly large ring, about the diameter of a tea plate. Inside the tube, she puts a few brightly coloured beads, or sequins, or small marbles that will roll properly and not stick. Before she heat seals the ends, she threads on some large wooden rings and some metal bangles. The result is a doodle toy which is full of interest to a child who can see a little, and it also has a pleasant feel.

A Flicky Windmill

Quick

Christine Cousins,
Educational Psychologist

Christine's flicky windmill is made from stiff cardboard (or thin plywood) cut in the shape of a cross. This is mounted on the flat top of a short piece of broomstick so that, when flicked, the blades easily rotate. The top surface is covered with diffraction paper which adds a touch of magic if the blades can be made to rotate in a strong light. Diffraction paper is available from Edu-Play (p. 187), and shops specialising in artists' materials. Alternatively, use diffraction stickers, sold individually from a strip at many toy shops, and costing only a few pence.

A Serendipity of Doodle Toys

Almost Instant – just allow a little time to collect them all!

Dr Lilli Nielson,
Danish expert on the
   education of visually
   handicapped children

Lilli Nielson has a magic suitcase full of bits and pieces guaranteed to please any child with a passion for doodling. Lift the lid and you will find:

- About four strings of beads and buttons, joined together at one end so that the loose ends form a tassle.
- Old bed springs, with the ends bent in and protected with plastic sticky tape.
- A pliable soap saver – the kind with drainage holes in the top, and covered with little plastic stickers on the reverse side.
- A bunch of real keys on a strong ring, with a wooden tag to dangle them by.
- An embroidery frame with tracing paper stretched tightly over it, making it like a flat little drum.
- An electric tooth brush holder (battery driven and without the brush) to switch on and off to experience the pleasant vibration.
- Three long strands of material, loosely plaited together, so that little fingers can wiggle between the strands.
- A bunch of bendy straws, taped together at the long ends, so that the bendy parts at the other end can be twisted about in different directions.
- Large buttons threaded on a loop of round elastic.
- Plenty of rattles, and tins to shake.

One can imagine any child saying to itself: 'Just let me get at that lot!'

MORE PLAY HELPS

Two Toys Using Chain

1. Chain in a Tin

*Almost Instant – just
    wait for the glue to dry*

Christine Cousins,
Educational Psychologist

This noisy doodle toy has instant child appeal. If you are familiar with the story of Winnie-the-Pooh and the chapter about Eeyore's birthday present, you will remember the delight he had lifting Piglet's popped balloon in and out of Pooh's empty honey jar. This toy seems to give children the same kind of soothing pleasure. It is made from three easily obtainable materials: a tin with a safe rolled edge, a length of metal chain and a blob of Araldite metal adhesive. The chain should be not more than a metre long, less if the child is small. Metal chain can be bought in ironmongers, builders' merchants and tool shops. The Araldite is required to anchor the chain to the bottom of the tin. When this has set, the toy is ready for use. If you want to stop the chain from disappearing inside the tin, tie a large ring (wider than the neck of the tin) to the free end. One from near the bottom of a Fisher Price stacking toy is ideal for the job.

2. Chain in a Bottle

Quick

Hettie Whitby,
Home Teacher of the Visually
    Handicapped

This version of the toy above uses a plastic bottle of the kind that has a handle moulded into it. In its first life, it will probably have contained fabric softener. This handle makes the bottle easy to hold and, when recycled as a toy, it is an excellent shape for the child to grasp with one hand while the other is busy manipulating the chain in and out of the neck of the bottle. In theory, the chain should stick to the bottom of the bottle with a blob of Araldite. I must confess mine came adrift. Perhaps the bottle was not completely dry inside. However, it was a simple matter to stitch the chain to the bottom of the bottle by poking a long needle threaded with button thread in one side, through the end link of chain, out the other side and under the bottom, repeating this loop several times.

I have made a few versions of this toy using various plastic bottles and different sorts of chain. They have all pleased the children. If the bottle is transparent, they can *see* what happens when they dangle the chain down the neck. If it is opaque, it can be a question of 'now you see it . . . now you don't!' and both can intrigue in their own way. The latest version has been made from a litre cooking oil bottle. This is transparent and has a very fat handle. An ingenious child can tip the bottle to make the chain travel through the handle before it emerges out of the neck.

A Custom Built Busy Board

Quick

Romayne Gayton,
Teacher of Visually
   Handicapped Children

Children at a certain stage of their development are intrigued by the activity boards now obtainable in a wide variety from all good toy shops. These are not always suitable for visually handicapped children who may be unable to see some of the items, e.g. the picture underneath the panel which slides to and fro, or the faces which appear in the little window when a knob is turned. Romayne has made a special busy board with none of these drawbacks. She has started with a base board in which holes have been drilled at random, but at least 6 cm apart. (Peg board can be used if some of the holes are ignored.) A short length of plasticised curtain wire is poked in one hole and out of another so that two stalks emerge from the base board. These need not be the same length. Something is threaded onto the stalks, and kept in place by beads glued to the cut ends of the wire. The process is repeated until the board is suitably filled. The items threaded onto the wire stalks can all come from the junk box. Romayne used various lids in which she had punched a hole; cotton reels of different shapes; hair curlers, both plastic and furry; size tags from coathangers given away by a large chain store; small threadable toys; and anything else that came to hand. The resulting busy board made a delightful toy. The pliable curtain wire could be pushed aside for the items threaded on it to be explored, and the beads on the ends knocked together when the wire was made to wobble about.

Materials
- A base board with holes in it
- Short lengths of plasticised spring curtain wire, probably about 22 cm long
- A selection of items to thread on the wire
- Large wooden beads to glue onto the cut ends

An Unusual Doodle Toy for a Blind Child

Quick

Hettie Whitby,
Home Teacher of the Visually
   Handicapped

Searching in the cupboard at Hounslow Toy Library for a suitable toy for a young blind child, Hettie came across a semicircle of wire mounted on a sturdy wooden base. In its better days, it had been decorated with large, brightly coloured beads which could be made to slide to and fro over the wire hoop. Now it was about to visit the repair box, for one end had become loose and it was only a matter of time before the remaining beads would come off and be lost. With a flash of inspiration Hettie could see a new life for the broken toy. With a little ingenuity, it could become a perfect plaything for the little girl she had in mind.

She removed the remaining beads and in their place threaded onto the wire hoop a nailbrush with a handle, some bracelets, a cat ball (like a golf practice ball with a bell inside) a saucepan brush with a long handle which had a convenient hole in it, and a couple of plastic rattles. The loose end of the hoop was poked back into the base board and wedged in firmly with a matchstick and plenty of glue. This strange 'toy' was now ready for a fresh start in life

The little girl was delighted with her new treasure and spent a long time exploring all its possibilities. She found that not only could she slide all the objects to and fro over the wire hoop, but the bracelets would slide over the cat ball, but not over the brushes. On the other hand, the saucepan brush on the long handle could be flicked from side to side . . . and so her exciting discoveries continued.

See also
Junk Toys to Hang Up for Children to Biff, Grab or Kick, p. 25

EXCITEMENT

'Surprise' toys are an excellent way of generating interest and excitement, and of focusing the child's attention on a particular spot. The sudden and unexpected change in what is seen can intrigue and amuse, as we all know when we play 'peep-bo' with a baby, holding our smiling faces (I defy anyone to take this game *seriously*!) behind our hands or the back of the chair. The same principle of 'now you see it – now you don't' is applied to many commercial toys and accounts for their popularity with children. A firm toy library favourite is the pop-up cone tree, and other toys like it, where the pieces are piled on top of a spring-loaded rod. When a button is pressed, the spring is released and the pieces pop up and scatter in all directions – an anticipated result which is usually repeated over and over again with much enjoyment.

Lots of children with special needs require this sort of surprise toy over a long period of time, and it can be difficult to find enough to ring the changes. This section offers five suggestions which should help. All are cheap, easy to make, and their inventors vouch for their success!

A Super Spectacular Instant Pop-up Dolly

Instant

Joan Thorpe,
Librarian,
Merry-go-round Toy Library,
Frimley

This is a splendid 'surprise' toy to use with any child who is at the 'looking' stage, *but* it must not be handled by the child without supervision.

Instant pop-up dollies have been around since the first edition of 'Play Helps'. They consist of the top half of a plastic bottle (washing-up liquid) and a dish mop! The handle of the mop is pushed inside the half bottle, and out through the neck, so that the fluffy part is completely hidden. Buttons, bells, colourful scraps of ribbon, etc.

59

are tied to the strands of the mop head which is made to pop in and out of the inverted bottle by pushing the handle up and down.

Joan has increased the excitement of this action by putting polystyrene 'chips' (the flat ones like potato crisps, used for packaging) or little bits of paper on top of the mop, so that when it is pushed up, a shower of pieces erupts, making the surprise even more spectacular.

A Peep-bo Toy

Quick

Catherine O'Neil,
Speech Therapist

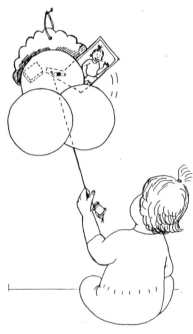

Here is a toy which certainly has excitement built into it! When not in use, it is colourful and attractive to look at, but pull the string, and WOW!

It is made from four circles of cardboard about the size of tea plates. These are coloured red, blue, green and yellow. Three are glued together in a group, overlapping each other. They provide a screen for the 'big surprise'. The fourth one, decorated in the drawing with a scalloped edge, acts as a backing piece. A matchbox and some glue are used to join it to the others as the final part of the construction. The holder for the 'surprise' is made from a separate piece of cardboard that can be made to pop up from behind the group of three circles when the string is pulled. It is oblong in shape, with a projecting tail which will always be hidden once it is fixed in place. The oblong is large enough to take a photograph or a picture postcard, i.e. about 100 x 160 mm. The tail is loosely fixed to the backing circle with a paper fastener, so that it is free to swivel. A string is tied to the far end of the tail so that when it is pulled downwards the picture pops up. Now is the time to glue the matchbox in position beyond the tail in such a way that it joins the backing piece to the group of circles, and acts as a spacer to allow room for the surprise piece to swivel freely. Make sure this is completely hidden before the string is pulled. Tie a cotton reel or a large bead to the end of the string to make it easier to hold. Mount the surprise picture on the oblong shape and you are ready for action. Use Blu-tack if you want to change the picture now and then.

Materials
- Cardboard
- Felt pens

- A paper fastener
- A matchbox
- String with a cotton reel on the end
- Photographs or pictures

A Peep-bo Puppet

Almost Instant

Mme Schneider,
Teacher of Visually
   Handicapped Children,
Switzerland

Here is an idea for a simple puppet which can be made in less than ten minutes! It is made in white material and decorated with black marker pen. This marked contrast between the colours used makes it stand out well from everything else in the room, and is therefore more likely to attract a child's attention.

All you need are two circles of white material, about 10 cm in diameter. Stick or sew them together for just over half the way round, leaving an opening at the bottom for your hand. Slip some card or stiff paper between the circles while you draw a face on both sides with a black marker pen. The card will prevent the ink from spreading through to the other side. Perhaps one face could be wide awake and the one on the opposite side asleep, or one face could be happy and the other sad. Put your fingers inside the head and use it to play peep-bo with your child. Make it appear over the back of a chair or peep from behind a curtain.

Pop-up Box

Quick

Jean Westmacott,
Lecturer,
Handicap Education and Aids
   Research Unit (HEARU),
City of London Polytechnic

This toy works on the same principle as a traditional see-saw. In its simplest form, this is just a plank of wood balanced over a fallen tree trunk. When one side goes down, the other rises. In the case of Jean's toy, a slot in the end of a box takes the place of the log, and the plank is now a strip of wood which balances in the slot. As the child pushes down his end (which is outside the box) the opposite one rises up to reveal the surprise fixed to the end of it.

The toy is made from an adult's shoebox. A slot is cut about two-thirds of the way up one end, and the strip of wood is pushed half way through this so that it balances. To stop it slipping about when weight is added to one end, glue a rounded surface to the underside of the wood, each side of the slot. There is room for experiment here. If the slot fits the wood fairly snugly, stumps of pencil may be enough to hold it in place. If you need something larger, try two rolls of thin cardboard. The lid of the box is placed in its usual position, but the part away from the child is cut away slightly to allow the surprise on the end of the see-saw to pop out. The rest of the lid hides the contents of the box nicely. If you remove your end of the box, you can change the surprises in secret!

What are these surprises? The choice is yours! Small toys can be fixed to the pop-up end with Blu-tack, or the pointed bit of cardboard that goes between the sections of an egg box can be stuck on to make a holder for a succession of finger puppets. (Make this cardboard spike lean slightly backwards so that when it pops out of the box it appears to be straight.)

Now play can begin. As the child lowers his end of the see-saw he can discover what you have attached to yours.

Materials
- An adult-sized shoebox
- A strip of wood for the see-saw
- Plenty of 'surprises'
- Ways of fixing them to the end of the wood (Blu-tack, masking tape, cardboard spike etc.)

Jean has used the Pop-up Box in a stronger form for a child who needed a toy he could work with his foot. His special box was larger and made of wood. The see-saw part had a foot pedal attached to the child's end, and a sloping dowel peg was fixed to the other. This was used to hold different glove puppets, which would pop out of the box when the foot pedal was depressed.

Lucky Bags

Quick

Mary Digby,
Play Specialist,
Moorfields Eye Hospital

Mary keeps a large supply of ready-filled Lucky Bags to add a touch of excitement to life in her ward. Any child undergoing an operation or lengthy treatment will be sure to find a Lucky Bag lurking under her pillow when she feels well enough to explore and find it. Lucky Bags are distributed generously throughout the day whenever the occasion merits a little celebration — perhaps as a reward for extra helpfulness or as a tiny prize for finishing a job well or winning a game. (The winner seems to have first pick, then everyone else has one too!) The bags are made by volunteers and filled with little surprises like a few marbles, a pair of doll's shoes or a dress, a miniature notebook and pencil, or some shells, the children never know what they might find!

FEELY TOYS

FUN

FEELY TOYS

Learning to use the sense of touch

Picture a baby in a high chair, impatiently waiting for his meal. His fat little palm starts to slap the cold plastic tray in front of him. He likes the *feel*, so he repeats the movement over and over again, sometimes using one hand, sometimes both, until his bowl appears. Lovely yummy cereal! He thinks: 'What will happen if I slap my palm in that?' We need follow the story no further! As he grows bigger, his natural curiosity and developing physical prowess will let him explore and investigate to his heart's content, touching, pulling, squeezing, pushing, pressing . . .

As we know, children with special needs are often unable to follow the normal pattern, so it is up to us to contrive ways of helping them to develop their sense of touch. It is easy to carry a small child around so that, during the course of his normal day, he can experience many different surfaces and textures. He can stroke the velvet curtains, pat the cold bathroom tiles, feel the cold water trickling out of the tap, the shape of your face and the texture of your clothes. Some of the slightly older children for whom this section is intended will find it difficult or even impossible, to explore for themselves and their hands may often be idle unless they have interesting tactile experiences brought to them. How can you know if you like the feel of velvet, or wet seaweed, if you have never had the chance to find out?

Just Feeling

All Instant or Quick

Alison Harland, who teaches in Hull, works with profoundly disabled children. She has found a new (and much more entertaining) use for the sponge plastic tubing normally used for pipe insulation. In her classroom several strips of this material are tied together, and are attached by elastic to a hook in the ceiling. Children in wheelchairs can be pushed through them to experience the feel of the long soft tubes passing over their bodies, or the wheelchairs can be positioned so the children can reach out and grab a piece, safely pulling it towards themselves, then letting go to make it bounce about at the end of its elastic.

Another idea of Alison's is to collect together several pairs of brightly-coloured pairs of tights, and tie them together to make an exotic octopus. Each leg is stuffed with a different 'feel'. This might be scrunched up newspaper, sponge pipe tubing, polystyrene chips, ping-pong balls etc. This wonderful creature can also be hung from the ceiling hook, but Alison found that just draping it over a couple of children so that they could play tug-of-war resulted in great hilarity!

Margaret Gilman, who is in charge of the nursery class at White Lodge Spastics Centre, has a more conventional octopus made from lots of strands of thick wool spread around a tennis ball. The wool is tied together at one end to make a top knot for the creature. The ball is pushed tightly against this and the strands of wool are arranged around it to cover the surface. Another length of wool is wound round, just below the ball to keep all the strands in place and form the 'neck'. Finally all the tentacles are made by plaiting the wool. This nice friendly octopus can be cuddled or waved about. Various small toys can be tied to the ends of his tentacles. He can then be hung up and used as a dangly toy holder.

Angela Smith, a teacher at Walton Leigh School (for children with severe learning difficulties), keeps in her cupboard an extra large bag, crammed to the top with tactile objects ready for the daily 'feely' session. She includes vinyl squeaky toys, soft toys, wooden objects, a small pillow case filled with rustling polystyrene chips, and things that feel cold, like a tin mug. She saves the plastic net bags from the greengrocer and fills them with anything that will intrigue the children, like milk bottle tops or pekan nuts. She also runs a neat line in the quickest and easiest feely bags it is possible to make! She collects odd socks, puts in a few acorns, or corks, or large buttons – whatever comes to hand – ties a knot in the top of the leg, and that is all there is to it!

Sylvia O'Bryan, a tutor on the Toy Making Course at the London College of Furniture, suggests stitching a soft piece of material (such as fur fabric) *inside* a child's pocket. Every time he puts his hand in, he will experience the pleasant texture.

She has also invented a gorgeous 'Amorphous Beanbag'. As its name suggests, it is a wholly unconventional shape which is, of course, its great attraction. The body of the beanbag is about the size of a tea plate, but the shape is anything but circular. At two places the material is extended into pairs of 'prongs' which narrow towards their ends and finish with dangling plaits of material or ribbon – lovely to slide between the fingers. The top of the bag is cut slightly larger than the bottom and a little pocket is made roughly in the centre, like the crater of a volcano! This is lined with fur fabric and the edge is gathered up with elastic so that an exploring finger can poke around inside. The beanbag is lightly stuffed with dried peas which can be manoeuvred in and out of the 'prongs'. Sylvia obviously has considerable needlework skills, but an Amorphous Beanbag (without the volcano pocket) is no more difficult to make than the conventional and uninteresting (one might even say *boring*) square or oblong shape. Think of a treasure island with lots of bays and peninsulas, and make a beanbag like that. The children will love it!

Four Rotating Feely Boxes

Long-lasting

Mathias Sarko and Saraspathy Sambasitam

Mathias Sarko from Ghana and Saraspathy Sambasitam from Malaysia invented a strong and interesting feely toy when they were students at the Handicap Education Aids Research Unit at the City of London Polytechnic. The descriptive title says it all. The four wooden boxes are similar in shape to Jusuf Raymond's Echo Blaster Windmill Dice. Please turn to p. 122 and examine the picture.

The feely boxes rotate around a length of thick dowel (or a broomstick), which is supported at both ends on a stand that raises them about a metre from the floor. This makes them the right height for a child in a wheelchair to reach conveniently. The sides of each box are covered with textures, and each one also makes a distinctive sound. The first contains rice, the second grit, and the other two, bells and marbles. The boxes are purposely made quite difficult to turn over. They cannot be flicked or made to spin round, but need a certain amount of pressure to make them rotate. The slight resistance makes the child press fairly firmly, and this helps him to be more aware of the textures on the box. The textures can be arranged as you wish, but here are some suggestions.

1. Every surface can have a different textural covering – a useful method if you are short of large pieces of material.
2. Each box can have the same covering on all its sides.
3. The same selection of textures can be used on every box so that one side of each will be the same. If this arrangement is used, the boxes can make a texture matching activity. Each box is rotated until there is a row of identical textures, like a much simplified version of Rubic's Cube, or the feely bricks on p. 68.

A Special Feely Cushion For Sarah

Quick

R.L.

Sarah, a little girl with severe handicaps, has many problems. She is not blind, but shows no interest in looking at anything. She is not deaf, but cannot speak and shows very little interest in sound. She has restricted movement in her limbs, and her days are spent for the most part in her special chair. Unless coaxed to hold something, her beautiful, elegant and unused hands stay resting on her lap. She seems to be living in her own little world, seldom even turning her head to notice her surroundings.

In an effort to please her, I decided to make a one-off lap cushion, and see what would happen. By chance, that morning I received a letter from Mme Schneider (from Switzerland) whose toys for visually handicapped children are included elsewhere. To get maximum colour contrast she uses black and white. The idea of making a toy in these colours was a new one to me, so

Sarah's cushion could be a good opportunity to try it out. A raid on the 'bits' bag produced some black satin and fur fabric. The satin was chosen for the top. This was decorated with four little attachments. One was made from a circle of white material, gathered round the edge like a mob cap and filled with small bells. Another was a long 'shocking pink' tube made from stretch velvet, and stuffed with marbles. It was attached to the cushion at both ends and resembled a handle. The marbles could be squeezed up and down the tube. The third attachment was made from brilliant green material and was shaped like a tree stump. It was filled with fish grit (used to cover the bottom of aquaria; cheap, and easy to buy from the pet shop). The last was made out of bright yellow fabric and stuffed with a 'Lanco' squeaky toy (p. 188) which would respond to the slightest pressure. The fur fabric was used for the bottom of the cushion, which was then stuffed with polystyrene chips to make a pleasant rustling sound if ever Sarah moved her hands. The fur fabric resting on her knees was intended to give her a warm, comfortable sensation, like nursing a friendly cat. Was it a success? How difficult it is to say! Certainly, Sarah's special cushion has been the only cuddly toy she has ever shown any interest in, and she seems to look for it, if for any reason she is parted from it. An act of faith perhaps, but she at least seemed satisfied with my efforts.

Following a Feely Trail

Quick

A Nursery School for Visually
    Handicapped Children,
Toronto

At this nursery school in Canada the children are taught to follow a feely trail with their finger tips. This is a good way of encouraging them to 'see' with their fingers, and is a preparation for learning to read Braille. A feely trail consists of a raised line which meanders across a sheet of cardboard e.g. the back of a Cornflakes packet. Usually several sheets are joined together to make a book. The raised surface can be made by first marking out the trail with a line of PVA adhesive and then pressing a piece of string onto it. The trail can go in any direction as long as it does not cross over itself and the more it twists and turns the more interesting and difficult it will be for the child to follow. String is not the only material that can be used. Anything that can be distinguished from the background is suitable. The list can include thick wool, piping cord or crochet cotton. As a further alternative, sand can be sprinkled on the glue trail, left to dry, and the surplus shaken off. The Canadian teachers have taken this last suggestion a stage further. For a really gritty feel, they use ground-up egg shells. These make a rough surface to the trail and are easily felt by children with a less developed sense of touch. Children who are good at following trails, press on this one gently – a desirable point where delicacy of touch is being encouraged. The egg shells are washed and the membrane linings removed. Then they are put through the mincing machine, or crushed with a rolling pin. The resulting fine grit can be used like glitter and sprinkled on the sticky trail. The surplus is shaken off. To make sure all the remaining pieces are well attached, another line of PVA adhesive can be added to the top of the trail.

We have a book of feely trails in the Kingston Toy Library. This has fairly heavy use and needs to be washed now and then, so it is made in fabric and the trails are stitched on. To give a little variety, piping cord, ric-rac braid and string are used on different pages. The early trails show a pipe cleaner child about to tread a wiggly path to a house made in materials of different textures; a bird taking an erratic flight to its nest in a tree; and a car about to drive around a bendy race track. The children with some sight find these pages particularly attractive. The other pages have snake-like patterns which increase in difficulty towards the end of the book. A button marks the start of each trail and a curtain ring indicates the end. All the buttons are on the top left hand corner of the page – the curtain rings can be anywhere!

Sorting and matching textures

Feely Bricks

Quick

R.L.

A set of feely bricks can be a useful addition to a collection of texture toys. Once they are neatly arranged in their box, all with the same texture uppermost, it is pleasant to run a hand over the surface and experience a large area of the same feel.

Make them from shabby Dean's Rag Bricks which have been well played with and often washed – they would welcome a face lift! (Or you can start afresh with cubes of foam plastic.) Because a cube has six sides, you need to select six materials with interesting textures. I used bubbly plastic, fur fabric, velvet, corduroy, PVC and denim. For a set of six bricks, cut six squares from each piece of material, the same size as the side of a cube. All six textures are used to cover each cube, so that every side has a different feel. Find a tray for the newly covered bricks – a cut-down cardboard box will do – and invite the child to place them in the tray, so that, for instance, all the velvet sides are on the top. Slow learners as well as children with a visual handicap enjoy this job. It does not matter if they recognise the materials by sight or touch. Either way, they will experience a pleasant tactile sensation as they stroke the tops of all the bricks when they are correctly placed in the tray.

Feely Gloves

Quick

Catherine Kent,
Teacher

Catherine, who works in a special school in Hull, uses cardboard hand shapes to make tactile pairs of 'gloves'. She draws round the children's hands, (good for body-awareness!), cuts out the shapes, and covers each pair with a textured material. The children can sort the 'gloves' into pairs and arrange them to fit their left and right hands. While doing this, they can experience the texture in front of them, and as they press their hands onto the glove shapes, they uncurl their fingers – to the satisfaction of the physiotherapist who is always urging them to 'make a flat hand'!

Glove Shops

Quick

R.L.

I used the same idea with two bright little six-year-olds, both of whom had recently lost their sight. As their home tutor, my brief was to help them to begin to adjust to their new way of life, and to teach them how to gather information through their fingers. We invented a game called 'Glove Shops'. First we had to make the stock, so we all made several pairs by drawing round our own hands on pieces of cardboard. For their first attempts, the children needed a little help in keeping the pencil vertical. The hand shapes were cut out for them, while they rootled in the 'bits' box for suitable material for the covering. They plastered the shapes with PVA adhesive, and stuck them to the reverse side of their chosen material. When the glue was dry, the glove shapes could be cut out. They could do this for themselves if the material was not too thick (so was easy to cut), because the cutting line round the edge of the card was easy to identify. At first, a few glove fingers needed repair, but the children gradually became more skilful. Next, a small hole was punched in the wrist of each glove, and the pairs were joined together with a treasury tag – useful practice in matching textures and threading. The pairs of gloves were conveniently priced at £1.00, £1.50 and £2.00, and were sorted into shoeboxes according to their 'value'. Then the shopping play began. In turn, each child was the shopkeeper, or bought gloves for all her family. Real money was used (and carefully sorted into piles at the end of the game) to give the children experience in distinguishing the shape and weight of the coins.

Families of Feely Dolls

Quick

A teacher in a school for children with severe learning difficulties was so taken with Loet's Instant Dolls (p. 50) that she started a small production line. She decided to make a host of dolls, so that they could be divided into the Velvet Family, the Hessian Family, the Cotton Family, etc. She invited her friends round for the evening and they all got busy! As the dolls were expected to receive plenty of handling, their clothes were both stuck and sewn. The storage problem was solved by making wall pockets to fit each family. Mr and Mrs Velvet lived in large velvet pockets, with smaller ones for the children and so on. At the end of playtime, returning the dolls to their proper places was a useful practical exercise in sorting and grading.

Feely Caterpillar

Quick

R.L.

One of these unusual creatures can be found in the cover picture. A series of little cushions joined together with Velcro create a floppy caterpillar rather like a concertina – head one end, tail the other. Toys made on the same principle are the 'Shake and Make' colour game (p. 47), and the 'Graded Caterpillar', (p. 79).

The original tactile version was made as a toy for visually handicapped children, so materials of a distinctive feel were used. It made a pleasant change from playing texture-matching games of Lotto or Dominoes. Collect together about six or seven pieces of material with distinctive characteristics (suggestions on p. 76). Using a saucer as a template, cut two circles from each type of material. Arrange the pairs of circles in a row so that those with a similar feel are not adjacent. Take the first pair of circles and stitch a face on one (two button eyes and a curtain ring mouth). Stitch a tail on the other and put it at the end of the line. Now roughly pin the remaining circles together in pairs so that the texture used for the back of the head will match the front of the next cushion and the back of this will match the front of the following one – and so on down the line until you end up with the tail attached to the back of the last cushion. Keeping the sequence intact unpin the circles and attach the Velcro by machine while the material is still flat. The Velcro must be sewn on correctly, e.g. furry sides to the backs of cushions and rough sides to the fronts. Now make up each cushion by placing the material right sides together, stitching round the edges, leaving a small opening for stuffing. Turn right sides out and stuff lightly before closing the opening. The cushions join together well if they are fairly flat and not too heavy.

Materials

- Textured fabric
- Saucer for template
- Velcro patches, cut from a strip
- Two buttons and a curtain ring for the face
- Wool tassel for the tail
- Small amount of stuffing (Acrylic or similar)

Giant Tactile Dominoes

Quick, Group (or individual child with adult)

Marie Madeline Reymond, Switzerland

The shoebox Giant Building Bricks described on p. 29 can easily be turned into huge dominoes which can be matched by touch. These make an excellent first texture-matching game for visually handicapped children, but it is also well worth making a set for any child who is beginning to use his sense of touch. At this stage, feeling is usually done with the whole of the inside of the hand, not just with the finger tips in the adult way. One half of a shoebox covered in a textured material offers a satisfyingly large surface to stroke.

The game is to place the boxes end-to-end in the correct order. This gives the children plenty of tactile experience and prepares them to play smaller commercial games of feely dominoes. Strengthen the shoeboxes by stuffing them with crumpled newspaper. (Extra weight can be added if you wish.) Tape on the lids. Sort out the textures you will use. (Consult the list on p. 76 for some suggestions if you need to seek inspiration!) Cover just the right half of the first box. Use the same material for the left half of the box that will follow it. The right half of this second box will correspond to the left half of the third one, and so on down the line. When you reach the final box, make its right half match the left half of the *first* box. Arranging the materials in this way means that, in play, the sequence of textures will always work, no matter which box is used to start the line i.e. (4/1 1/2 2/3 3/4 etc.).

Feely boxes

Feely boxes seem to appeal to every child who is at the right age to appreciate uncertainty and surprise. In my youth, the bran tub at the local fête was always surrounded by a crowd of children eager to fish around in the bran to see what they could find. Bran tubs with their special smell and feel seem to have been replaced by lucky dips which are often no more than a bucket full of colourfully wrapped little bundles. Certainly, these are less messy, but the presents are not *hidden*, so they completely miss out on the mystery and excitement of the old bran tub. Never mind! The following ideas can bring back some of that old excitement. These feely boxes keep their contents secret, so the children must make their choice by feel and not by sight.

Two Cheap and Easy to Make Feely Boxes

1. *Instant*

Nina Hanson,
Humberside Toy Libraries

Use a strong cardboard carton. (The sort that usually holds whisky bottles is ideal.) Put this in an old stretch nylon cushion cover. The elasticated opening in this will gather nicely round the top of the box, leaving a hole to dip into.

2. *Quick*

Nursery Nurses,
Bedelsford School

This feely box is also made from a carton. If it has flaps for a lid, turn it upside down (flaps now at the bottom). Cut two round holes in the new top, fairly near to one side, (i.e. not in the centre). These are for the child's arms to reach into the box. On the opposite side, where you will sit, cut a door flap so that you can change over the items in the box. You are now ready for action. Your child puts his hand through the holes in the top. You lift the flap and maybe pop in a square brick. When this is successfully identified, it might be exchanged for a ball or a soft toy. The choice is yours. At a later stage, it is fun to put several things in the box. By using only his sense of touch, the child must pick out one object from among many.

If this feely box is to be used more than a few times, it is worth while making it look more attractive by covering the sides with wrapping paper or a collage of old Christmas cards stuck on at random. It is best not to decorate the top. Pictures here could distract the child from the job in hand, which is thinking about what he is examining by touch.

As an added refinement, stick a cotton reel knob onto the flap to act as a handle and make it easy to lift.

Shake Hands Feely Box

Instant

Noah's Ark Toy Library,
Melbourne,
Australia

Here is a variation on the above ideas. Two children sit each side of a cardboard box which has a hole cut in each end, and reach inside until their hands touch. They usually find this unseen contact hilarious! Then a hand shaking ritual takes place.

Footnote. This is fine for children who do not shrink from physical contact, but for some, it would be a far from amusing experience. A small autistic member of a toy library was in this position. Once his buggy was outgrown, the only way of keeping him safe in the street was to make him wear a harness and reins. His mother managed gradually to overcome his fear of holding hands by playing various clapping games with him. Through these he made brief contact with another person's hands and, in time, consented to have his held. His mother made up little chants like 'Clap, clap together, clap, clap to Daddy' while she stood behind him, gently holding his wrists and controlling his hands. His father faced him, demonstrating the appropriate actions. It was easier to hold the child's interest if the words were sung to a simple tune.

The Treasure Chest

*Instant except for
    collecting the treasure*

Nina Hanson,
Humberside Toy Libraries

This is a lucky dip game in which the sighted players must either be trusted to keep their eyes shut, or be provided with a blindfold. The idea is that fingers should do the work of eyes, and that the objects taken from the treasure chest should be identified solely by the sense of touch. When the child has made his guess, he can check it by opening his eyes or removing the blindfold.

Any container will do for the treasure chest (e.g. either of the feely boxes above). The treasure could consist of a crown from the dressing-up box, a purse or two, necklaces, bracelets, rings etc. Add to the enjoyment by telling a story about explorers landing on a desert island and produce the treasure chest as the punch line.

Story Books with a
    Magic Touch

Quick

Mary Digby,
Play Specialist,
Moorfields Eye Hospital

On our toy library shelves, you will find feely books made by me containing collage pictures using materials with different textures. These are fine as far as they go, but I have a feeling they sometimes appeal more to the parents than to the children! Mary Digby has found a way to lift the whole idea onto a more child-centred plane. She and her students make story books that relate to *real life* situations. They are illustrated with *real* objects, which can be touched, and sometimes smelt, as the story unfolds. Each book contains approximately eight pages, and tells about a little girl called Jenny who does ordinary things like 'Visiting Granny'. In this particular story, page 1 describes her being smartened up for the occasion. Alongside the writing, the page contains a *flannel* and *soap, comb, Noddy toothbrush*, and a *nail brush*. They are all stuck, with Araldite, to a thick cardboard page. (In spite of much handling, they are still there!)

On page 2, Jenny's mother makes her own preparations. She gives Jenny her spectacles to clean, while she packs her handbag for the day, putting in her diary, watch, handkerchief, comb, purse with money in it and a bunch of keys. All these are mounted on the page.

By page 3, she is finishing her preparations and takes the rollers out of her hair, puts in her hair clips, chooses a necklace to wear, and applies her perfume.

Page 4 describes Jenny playing with a Bendy doll while she waits for her mother. During her play, a button falls off her coat.

By page 5, they have arrived at Granny's. They walk over the pebbles on the path, smell the lavender bush and examine the sea shells round the door.

On page 6 Granny notices the missing button. She finds her thimble, needlebook and some thread. She takes her glasses out of the case and sews on the button.

Now it is time for lunch, so on page 7 Jenny lays the table with a knife, fork, spoon and a paper plate. She arranges the plastic flowers to put in the middle.

The final page is all about going home. Granny, true to type, gives Jenny some good-bye presents: a purse with coins in it, some sweets, a balloon and a pen.

In another volume Jenny visits Moorfields Eye Hospital, and the book describes the activities of the ward, and how the children spend the day – the toys they use and the games they play. Further pages show the toilet articles on the locker and the equipment for a visit to the Operating Theatre. Breakfast the next day will include an individual pack of Rice Krispies, a bendy straw and tomato ketchup in a packet! After all the details about the morning's treatment, the book ends on a happy note with a picture Bingo board and all the cards to match to it, and of course a Lucky Bag prize for winning!

Other titles include *Jenny Goes to a Birthday Party, Jenny Spends the Night at Granny's House*, and *Jenny Goes on Holiday to Hungary*. This last one includes details of the flight and staying in an hotel.

With all the lumpy articles stuck to each page these delightful feely books are obviously quite thick. The stout cardboard pages have holes punched on one side and are tied together loosely with string.

Materials with Interesting Textures

- Artificial grass – as seen at the greengrocers
- Blanket
- Brushed nylon or cotton
- Bubbly plastic
- Carpet samples
- Chain; metal from an ironmonger, plastic from a garden centre
- Coarse tweed
- Corduroy
- Embossed wallpaper
- Felt
- Fluted cardboard
- Fur fabric, long and short pile
- Needlecord
- Nylon netting
- Nylon deck chair canvas
- Plastic foam
- PVC
- Prickly doormat
- Rug canvas
- Velvet
- Vivelle (felt flocked paper, obtainable from educational suppliers)

See also
Hotch Potch of Suggestions for Toys and Other Objects to Suspend, p. 7
Tactile Posting Box, p. 130

FUN

Monster Toast

Instant

Joan Thorpe,
Librarian,
Merry-go-round Toy Library,
Frimley

Here is a lovely idea from America, passed on by Joan. To make monster toast, paint a face on a slice of bread, using edible colouring. If the bread has holes in it, so much the better. Turn these into a mouth and eyes to create the 'monster'. Then toast, butter and EAT!

Note. Make sure the colouring is safely edible. Remember some children have allergies.

Instant Hats

Quick

Pam Rigley,
Toy Librarian,
Reading

What can be more fun than dressing-up or going to a party?

Pam has contributed the patterns for paper hats which are eminently suitable for both these activities. The basic patterns are very little trouble to make, (I have tried them out!) and, of course, can be elaborated if you feel in the mood. It is best to make a prototype first in newspaper. With a rough sample in front of you, it is a simple matter to go into mass production if you need to. The size suggested should be right for the average five-year-old, but we all know there is no such thing as an average child. Your prototype can come in handy as a check on the measurements, and you can adapt accordingly.

Petal Hat

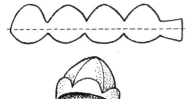

Cut a strip of paper approximately 580 x 250 mm. Fold it in half. Mark off 60 mm from one end. This will make the tab for joining the finished hat together. Disregarding this 60 mm, fold the rest of the strip into four to make the four petals. Shape the petals by rounding off the open ends. (Do *not* cut through the fold.) Open out the paper and refold, so that it resembles the diagram, with a small petal slightly overlapping a large one. Trim the tab to a suitable size and fix the hat together with a staple or glue. Join the tips of the large petals together to form the crown. (Glue is easier than stapling.)

Bonnet or Halo

You need a piece of paper about 420 x 520 mm, roughly the size of a wallpaper sample. Fold it in half to bring the short sides together. Cut out on the dotted lines as in the diagram. Thread a ribbon along the inside of the fold for tying under the chin. Staple it in place. The half moon shape inside the halo can stay as it is, or be folded back to stand upright behind the head.

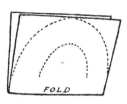 

Fringed Helmet

Use a piece of paper approximately 600 mm square. Cut down the dotted line as in the diagram to within about 100 mm of the lower edge. Wrap it round to fit the child's head, and staple in position. Tie a band around the top half of the fringe to make a plume which hangs down the back. Because the part that fits round the head is only a single thickness of paper, a strengthening strip of Sellotape around the inside of the lower edge is a good idea.

Origami Hat

This is made from a double page of a full-sized newspaper. Fold over the double page from top to bottom, and fold in the top corners so that they meet in the middle. Fold up the two front edges and crease firmly. Turn the hat over and turn up the two back edges to match. Staple or stick the edges together.

See also

Hopefully, the whole of this book! But especially:

GRADING

GRASP AND RELEASE

GRADING

A Graded Caterpillar

Quick

R.L.

This weird and wonderful creature, unknown to any naturalist, consists of a series of circular felt cushions, graded in size between the largest for the head to the smallest for the tail. The segments are joined together with Velcro, giving the assembled creature a concertina-like appearance. It makes an excellent toy for slow learners, and for children with hand function problems. At first, they enjoy just pulling all the bits apart; then they can learn to figure out how to join all the pieces together again. Adult help is needed here until the child realises that the rough strip (or spot) of Velcro will only stick to the furry Velcro strip on another segment. Joining just two segments together can be a satisfying experience for some children, others will like to put all the pieces in order and so make a presentable caterpillar.

Materials
- Felt, the choice of colour is yours
- A little polyester fibre, or similar – for stuffing
- Scraps of different coloured felt to make a face on the front of the largest segment
- Scraps of wool to make a tassel tail for the back of the smallest segment
- Velcro, either cut from a strip or 'Spot-ons'

Method
Begin with the tail. Cut two circles of felt about 60 mm in diameter. Sew these together and stuff lightly. Stitch one half of a piece of Velcro to one side and a wool tassel to the other. Make the next segment about 90 mm in

diameter, stuff it, and add the other half of the tail Velcro to one side and a new piece to the other. Remember, from now on each segment must have one rough and one furry piece. Continue to make more segments, each 30 mm larger than the previous one, until the caterpillar is the length you want. Six segments is a popular size. Finish off the front of the largest segment with a happy face made from scraps of felt (or buttons?).

A Circle Matching and Grading Activity

Very quick

R.L.

One day, while working at a school for children with severe learning difficulties, I noticed a little boy crouching in the corner of the playground. His attention was totally absorbed by a plastic bucket filled to the brim with bottle tops of every shape and size, which he was busily arranging in patterns and groups. Sometimes he put all those of one size together, then he would arrange them in a long line. Some might be piled on top of each other, or one might be hidden under another one. Whoever thought up this inspired 'toy' had provided the little boy with hours of happy play.

This incident suggested to me the idea of using plastic lids to make a grading toy. All the staff were asked to save the lids and bottle tops (without sharp edges) they would normally throw away. By the end of the week there was a fine selection, ranging in size from the caps from tubes of toothpaste to lids from large tins of emulsion paint. When they were all cleaned up, the only thing they had in common was their circular shape!

This is how the grading toy was gradually invented. At first, we offered the box of lids to the children as a toy to see what they might think of doing with them. Most were at a loss to know where to begin, so we thought a quickly made matching game might help. Five lids were chosen, ranging from very small to very large. These were outlined at random on a large sheet of paper, and the outlines coloured in with a marker pen. Each lid could now be matched to its silhouette. Then more circles were added to the paper to make the difference in size less marked. This could cause problems if a child was working on his own, for a large lid could easily cover a small circle, and after a few had been covered, some remained with no lid big enough to hide them. We found that if the circles were arranged in line, with the smallest first and the size gradually increasing, the children found it easier to move the lids up and down the line to find the correct match. The nearer they were in size, the more carefully the children had to look to make sure all the circles were properly covered.

Finally, we hit on the idea of adding an element of fun to the box full of lids. One break time all the teachers were asked to draw a picture where lots of circles were part of the design, using the lids as templates. The idea was that the children should match them to parts of a picture — surely a more attractive proposition than just covering circles in a row! The quickly-drawn pictures were later coloured in and mounted on card to make them last longer. They turned out to be an absorbing activity in great demand at 'Choosing Time'. One picture was of a lorry. Lids could cover the wheels, the steering wheel and the different circular objects that made up the load. Other ideas were a ship, with portholes to cover and a row of circular waves for it to float on; an herbaceous border with the centres of the flowers to be filled in; a coat with an odd assortment of buttons down the front; a park full of round 'lollipop' trees in varying stages of growth, and a picture of a child blowing bubbles.

See also
Families of Feely Dolls, p. 70

GRASP AND RELEASE

A New Use for the Soft Woolly Ball

Quick

R.L.

Peter was a lad with cerebral palsy. Like many other such children he had great difficulty in letting go of an object once his fingers were clasped tightly round it. His Physiotherapist asked me to devise a toy which would encourage him to pick something up, extend his arm and then release the object. What seemed to be needed was an oversize posting box with only one hole. After a quick survey of all the scrap materials available, a plastic sweet jar was chosen to be the container. This had a wide neck which made a good target to aim for. The jar was also transparent, so seeing the results of his efforts as he gradually filled it up should give Peter some 'job satisfaction'.

The next problem was how to keep the jar stable, for in its empty state it was large and very light, and consequently easy to knock over. The problem was a simple one to solve. A few stones were placed in the bottom of the jar. They were then covered with Polyfilla, mixed to a consistency which was just sloppy enough to settle between them. When this had set, the plastic jar had a permanently weighted base. Now all that was needed was something suitable to drop into it. Tennis balls were the ideal size to fit Peter's hand, but when using these, his jerky movements would scatter them to the four corners of the room. The solution proved to be a generous supply of our old friends, soft woolly balls, stored in a plastic bowl resting on a Dycem mat.

For anyone who has missed out on making soft woolly balls in their youth, here is how to set about it.

Cut two identical circles of card from a Cornflakes packet, using a saucer as a template. Cut a hole in the centre of each, this time using a wine glass to give the size. Put the pieces of card together and wind brightly coloured wool over the edge and up through the middle, gradually covering the cardboard ring with wool until the central hole is quite filled in. (If you hold it up to your eye, you shouldn't be able to see through it.) Take a sharp pair of pointed scissors and at one place on the circumference of the circle snip the wool until you reach the cardboard. Then poke the scissors between the pieces of card and continue cutting all round. You now have lots of strands of wool sticking out each side of the cardboard circles. Using *strong button thread*, part the cards a little way and *tightly* wind the thread between them, finishing off with a sturdy knot. This holds all the strands of wool firmly together, and the cardboard circles can be removed. Fluff up the wool to make the ball a good shape, and trim off any odd ends that stick out.

Drainpipe Skittles

Instant

Brian Spencer,
Remedial Gymnast,
The Manor Hospital

Games of skittles are very popular with the hospital residents and are a useful form of exercise when the weather prevents outdoor activities. For those who are unable to bowl at the skittles in the normal way, Brian provides short lengths of drain pipe which can guide the ball in the right direction. Using this simple aiming device, all the player has to do is to release the bowling ball when he judges the pipe to be pointing in the right direction, and it will travel down the pipe and, hopefully, scatter the skittles. Brian finds that a sweet placed on top of a particular skittle considerably increases the player's concentration and skill – and his enjoyment if he knocks off the sweet and is entitled to eat it!

Drop It In

Instant

Pam Courtney,
Deputy Head Teacher,
St Anne's School

In a large cardboard carton Pam stores a collection of different containers. These include a cake tin, plastic bowls of different sizes, a coffee tin, a wooden box, a plastic ice cream tub etc. She also has a variety of objects which can be put in them. She uses plastic and metal spoons, pasta shells, cotton reels, fir cones, stones, woolly balls – in fact, anything that can ultimately be sorted into groups. At first, the children just put anything into anything! Later on they learn to sort the objects into groups, then put them into specific containers. Dropping a metal spoon into a cake tin will make a lovely clatter, and besides being fun, it practises the action of grasping and releasing. It *can* lead on to tidy habits, and putting things in their correct place. All desirable objectives.

See also
Higher and Higher, p. 154
A Tropical Aquarium, p. 156
Stack Anything, p. 157

HANDS

Which Way Does it Go?

Long-lasting

Annie-Marie Jucker,
Physiotherapist,
Switzerland

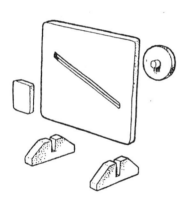

Anne-Marie has made a strong and useful piece of apparatus to help children to control their hand and finger movements. It looks so attractive that it certainly counts as a toy!

She has painted a series of pictures on both sides of pieces of plywood illustrating summer and winter scenes. The pictures are supported on two wooden feet. Each picture has a small 'object' associated with it. This is painted on a separate piece of plywood, and moves along a slot (or rotates in a hole) cut out of the main picture. For example, the kite moves *up* into the sky, the boat sails *across* the lake, the snowball rolls *down* the mountain and the bee buzzes *round* the flower. Each object is fixed to another on the opposite side of the slot (or hole) by means of a short length of dowel.

The therapist makes up a story about the picture and encourages the child to take part by moving the object in the right direction, giving a little help if necessary from her side of the board.

The pictures are simple and uncluttered. Apart from their primary purpose, they can be used to illustrate concepts such as up and down, large and small, etc. For children who have not yet reached this stage, the scenes are interesting to watch as the therapist activates the moving part.

Materials
- Four pieces of plywood for the pictures; suggested size 400 x 400 mm with a thickness of 6 or 8 mm.
- Extra plywood for the moving parts.

continued on p. 86

Materials (*continued*)
- Four short lengths of dowel for joining these together.
- Wood for the feet; suggested size for each foot is 200 mm long, 20 mm wide and 100 mm high.
- Gouache paints for the pictures.
- Polyurethane varnish; a coat or two for a protective covering.

Hand-prints

Quick

People who work and play with brain-damaged children are often looking for new ways of helping them to realise where they can find the different parts of their body, and which bit does what! Making a hand- (or foot) print is one way of focusing a child's attention on that extremity. Hands can be smeared in a tray of paint and then used to print their shape on a piece of paper. Better still, each hand can be placed flat on the paper while you draw around it. The child can take his time, flattening out his hand and spreading his fingers. Then comes the best bit when he experiences a lovely tingly feeling as your pencil traces round the outline. Try it!

Hand-prints are often cut out and used as a classroom decoration. At Linden Bennet School each child in a class makes several pairs of hand-prints and a pair of foot-prints. These are cut out and arranged on large sheets of poster paper as giant flowers. The footprints, together with a photograph of the child's face, go in the centre of the flower, and the hand-prints are arranged all around to make the petals.

At Dysart School the body of a large bird is drawn on sugar paper, and the outline is filled in with overlapping hand-prints, pointing towards the tail, to represent the feathers.

At other schools, cut-out hand-prints are used to make very effective trees. In the Autumn, the hand-prints can be made in yellow, orange and brown to represent the autumn tints, and a cluster of hand-prints can be arranged in a tree shape with the fingers pointing upwards. When December comes, more hand-prints can be made in dark green, and arranged as a Christmas tree, this time with the fingers pointing down.

Flaccid hands

Here are some suggestions which could be helpful to children who find it difficult to grasp, press or pull.

Just Pulling

Instant

Christine Cousins,
Educational Psychologist

1. Present the child with a square box of tissues – the decorative kind usually found on dressing tables. Let her pull the tissues out one by one, through the hole in the centre of the lid. Collect the tissues up for future use or for a game of tug of war with big brother!

2. Start off with a polythene ice cream container. Make a small hole in the lid. String together many strips of material. (Make sure the knots will go through the hole in the lid.) Put all the material neatly in the container, thread one end through the hole, put the lid on securely and invite the child to start pulling. She will be amazed at the seemingly endless string of material she is producing and will surely be motivated to carry on to the bitter end! This toy reminds me of the yards of silk handkerchieves magicians can produce from the most unlikely places.

One Hole Posting Boxes

Quick

Teachers at the Sense
   Centre for Deaf/Blind
   Children

At the Centre, teachers have collected a variety of posting boxes, each with a hole cut in its polythene lid. They have made sure that the items to be posted are *slightly* larger than the holes through which they are to be pushed. This makes certain that the child must exert some pressure to achieve the satisfying plop of a successful posting. The children begin with the tin which

87

takes a ping-pong ball. When they can manage this, they try another tin with a smaller hole and a different object to post – perhaps a wooden bead. A cylindrical shape is harder to line up than a sphere, so the next stage is to move on to the tin which takes a plastic hair curler end on. This has small plastic bristles which rub against the sides of the circle cut in the polythene lid. Some adults hate the sound and feel of this, but the children *love* it!

Stroking

Children who find it difficult to keep their fingers straight are often encouraged to make a stroking action. Here are two suggestions for play ways of achieving this movement.

Make a Fur Fabric Caterpillar

Quick

These were all the rage a few years ago, but now seem to have disappeared from the shops. They are simplicity itself to make. Just cut a strip of fur fabric about 240 mm x 80 mm, making sure the pile runs the length of the strip. The caterpillar rests on your arm, or upper leg if you are in a wheelchair, with the pile of the fur lying in the direction away from your body. As you stroke along the lie of the pile, the caterpillar will hump himself up your arm (or leg) in a realistic manner. He can be given character by adding eyes and a smiling mouth. Embroider them in wool or stick on tiny pieces of felt.

Make a Paint Sandwich

Quick

This is an alternative to finger painting and is considerably less messy. The bread part of the sandwich is made from cling film. A strip of this thin plastic film is placed on the table and a few blobs of thick paint (finger paint or powder mixed with a little Gloy) are dotted here and there. Use different colours for maximum enjoyment. Another layer of cling film is carefully laid on top, avoiding creases, and (hopefully) sealing the paint within the sandwich. Using a flat hand, the child can stroke the blobs of paint and spread them out within the sandwich, blending the colours together to make interesting effects.

Using both hands

Throw and Catch

Instant

Christine Cousins,
Educational Psychologist

Christine has invented a throwing game in reverse. In this version of 'throw and catch', *you* do the throwing while the child receives your missile in a cardboard carton! This needs to be held firmly in *both hands* while objects of different weights are thrown into it to land on the bottom with a satisfying thump.

A New Use for a Salad Dryer

Instant

Linda Rhead,
Head Teacher,
Bedelsford School

Here is an original idea which has been a proven success with autistic children, and is also a valuable way of encouraging a child to use both hands. All it needs is a rotary salad dryer and a few things to put in it. Try using a few marbles, or wooden beads or even butter beans (raw). Each of these will make a different sound and offer a different resistance to the handle of the salad dryer. For big results, all the child has to do is to clasp the dryer firmly to his chest, and turn the handle vigorously!

Marble Tray Painting

Instant

Stephanie Clements,
Teacher,
Bedelsford School

Stephanie has several children with cerebral palsy in her class. Marble tray painting is one of their favourite double-handed activities. For this she uses a round tin tray with a high lip, and lines the bottom with a circle of paper. The chosen child drops a few blobs of paint on the paper, then rolls a couple of marbles around on the tray to spread the paint in a delicate trail. If you like this idea, but don't have a tin tray handy, the bottom of a bucket will do just as well.

Zanna's Plonk Pads

Quick

R.L.

One of the children in a Special Care Unit had a distressing habit of biting her thumb whenever she was left to her own devices. Her teacher tried various ways of keeping her hands occupied and away from her teeth, but success was patchy. The only sure solution was one-to-one attention, but with a room full of other equally handicapped children that was, of course, impossible. The girl liked to pull at the Velcro joining the fronts of her jacket together, and this gave me the clue to the invention of a 'toy' which made use of this useful fastening, and might be a means of keeping her hands occupied. A couple of small oblong cushions were made, like shoe polishing pads, the right size to fit the girl's hands comfortably. A long strip of Velcro was sewn down the middle of each so they could be endlessly pressed together, then pulled apart, making the rending sound she enjoyed. A strip of elastic was sewn across the back of each pad to help the girl to hold them more easily. Her fingers were slipped under the elastic which rested across the backs of her hands. This queer 'toy' was called Zanna's Plonk Pads! It met with qualified success once the novelty of it had worn off. However, it led to the creation of the next toy which has had an enthusiastic reception at the toy library!

Popper Balls

Quick

R.L.

This toy consists of a bag full of a dozen brightly coloured felt balls, all the same size (rather smaller than a tennis ball). Each one is fitted with a Velcro Spot-on. (Velcro in the form of a spot instead of the usual strip. These spots are sold at haberdashery departments in large stores, and handicraft shops.) Every ball is made from six sections of felt, each cut like the petal of a flower. The sections are 90 mm long and 30 mm across at the widest part. When the ball is stuffed, one half of a Velcro Spot-on is sewn to the North Pole, the other half to the South. With a little careful arrangement to make sure that a furry Velcro surface is pressed to a rough one, all the balls can be made to stick together. Most children discover the trick of linking the surfaces by trial and error.

The toy library parents who borrow the balls tell me they use them in many ways. One piles them on her baby's legs for her to kick away, another rolls them around the floor for her son to crawl after. The balls can be joined together, then pulled apart by a child – like pulling a cracker. Older children can match the colours, then join the balls together in pairs, or the whole lot can be stuck together to form a circle and can be worn as an oversize necklace. There is no danger of strangulation; if the necklace is pulled, the Velcro spots split apart.

As the balls are made of felt, they are not washable, so sometimes need a trip to the dry cleaners.

Materials and Method
- A cardboard template for cutting all the sections. Draw an oblong, 90 mm x 30 mm. Mark the centre of each side with a cross. Draw a petal shape which touches all four crosses, and cut it out.
- Coloured felt in different colours.
- Polyester fibre for the stuffing.
- A Velcro Spot-on for each ball.

Cooperation Game

Quick

Linda Rhead,
Head Teacher,
Bedelsford School

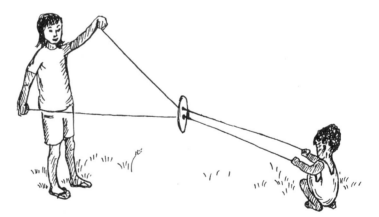

In this game a disc of plywood about the size of a dinner plate is made to pass 'to and fro' between two players holding the ends of two lengths of cord threaded through it. When their arms are relaxed nothing happens. The cords just sag in the middle, but if the cords are held taut and player 'A' opens his arms, he will slide the disc towards his partner 'B'. Then the process is reversed and the disc slides back. The children soon learn that if both open their arms together there is stalemate!

91

The game should be played with both players standing up, but if this proves difficult try letting the receiver crouch down while the sender opens his arms to send the disc along the cord which is now a downhill slope. For the return journey the players reverse positions.

Materials and Method

- A circle of plywood. Draw the diameter and on this drill two holes – like holes in a button.
- Nylon cord. This is the most suitable, because it is strong and slippery. Its length is optional, but about two metres for each piece is suggested.
- Four handles to attach to the ends of the cords after they have been threaded through the holes.

Recipes for Play Pastry

Uncooked

2 cups salt
2 cups flour
Enough water to mix a stiff dough

This dough will keep quite happily for at least a week if stored in a container in the fridge between playtimes. A few drops of food colouring or powder paint can be added to the mixing water if desired.

Cooked

1 cup plain flour
½ cup salt
2 tsp cream of tartar
1 tbs cooking oil
1 cup water

Cook slowly until very hot. The mixture gradually comes away from the sides of the pan. When cool, it makes a delightfully soft dough which is pleasant to handle and will not dry the children's hands. Stored in the refrigerator, it stays fresh longer than the uncooked version.

A Surprising Substance

1 part cornflour
1 part salt
1 part water

This recipe will make an extraordinary mixture. It can be dribbled over the children's hands, or dropped onto a

Formica-topped table and pushed into all sorts of shapes, only to regain its original position seconds later.

Icing Sugar Play Dough

Quick

Fiona Priest,
Therapist,
Honeylands

As a very special treat, Fiona suggests modelling with icing sugar mixed with a tiny amount of egg white, and perhaps a drop or two of food colouring or peppermint essence. The resulting 'play dough' has one great advantage over the flour and salt recipes: the chances are that most of it will have disappeared before the end of the session! If the children's appetites can be restrained, they can make sugar mice by rolling the dough into the shape of a fat sausage, pinching out a nose, face and two little ears and inserting two currant eyes and a string tail. Snowmen are also popular. Make one from two sugar dough balls, one large, one small. Two currants and a small piece of glacé cherry make the face. Finish him off with a row of currant buttons down his front. If they survive that long, these snowmen (or mice) make good Christmas presents for one child to give to another.

A Fishing Game That Will Last

Quick

Pat Kelly,
Parent,
Howgill Centre,
Whitehaven

Catching cardboard fish with a magnet at the end of a line is a delightful game which has been enjoyed by generations of children. Apart from being fun, it has its useful side too. It helps to practise hand-eye coordination and encourages concentration and persistence.

There are several attractive fishing games on the market and these are good as a game for frail children where a low effort toy is needed. But they have disadvantages. The pond is usually nothing more than a four-sided cardboard tube which will squash flat to fit in the box; the fish are small and insufficient in number; the rods are thin; and the magnets at the end of the line are adequate for the job providing they are dropped exactly onto the right part of the fish. All this can add up to a heap of frustration for a child who needs a more robust toy he can handle with confidence.

By far the best fishing games are the home-made ones! They can be made a sensible size, so that the fish are easy to see and handle. A strong magnet will lift the fish, even if it doesn't drop in exactly the right place. The length of the line can be adjusted to fit the child's skill — the shorter the line, the easier it is to land a fish.

The game made by Pat used a large plastic ice cream tub as a pond. The outside was decorated with buckets and spades, boats, seaweed etc., so that the children could associate it with the seaside. A steel paper clip was attached to the 'nose' of each fish. The fishing rods were made of dowel, and the one for a disabled child had a bicycle handle bar grip slipped over the end to make it easier to hold. The magnet used was a strong circular one with a hole in the middle (obtainable from some hardware or tool shops, or from Educational Suppliers, p. 187). At the end of the game, all the bits and pieces could be stored in the 'pond'.

It is suggested you use only one magnet. If two children play at the same time, the magnets attract each other and the lines are constantly entangling. It is best to make the game a turn-taking one. When a child has caught a fish, he hands the rod to the next player.

Materials
- A plastic container.
- Cardboard for the fish.
- Felt pens to colour them.
- Steel paper clips (*see* note below).
- A fishing rod made from a short length of dowel (the handle of the washing-up mop will do).
- A sturdy line.
- A strong magnet. This is the most expensive part of the toy.

An important note on steel paper clips
Pat used the ordinary domestic curly wire ones, easily obtainable from any stationers. Her game was used only under supervision, and with children who were not able to remove the clips from the fish. A safer clip to use is known as a 'daisy clip'. It has a flat circular steel eye, and two steel 'legs' which can be poked through several pieces of paper, then opened out to keep them all in place. These large paper fasteners are obtainable from major suppliers of office stationery. We have a popular fishing game in the Kingston Toy Library which uses them for the fishes' eyes. Every fish shape is cut out twice. A 'daisy clip' is pushed into each, and the prongs are flattened out at the back. Both halves are stuck

together with strong glue, (Evostick, or similar, with lots round the edges to deter the children from 'picking' the fish apart!) The steel prongs are safely encased in the body of the fish.

See also
Just Feeling, p. 64
Four Rotating Feely Boxes, p. 65
A Special Feely Cushion for Sarah, p. 66
Feely Gloves, p. 69
Rock and Roll Tumble Balls, p. 139
Threading, pp. 158–160
Fingerplay Books, p. 186

IMAGINATION

Let's pretend

How children love this kind of play, and how splendidly it encourages the use of the imagination – especially when the 'props' are not too realistic. I vividly remember the days of my early childhood, spent on the Isle of Wight with a safe sandy bay as a playground, when my friend and I would spend hours playing 'shops' on the beach. This was long before the era of supermarkets. The shops in our village all had an impressive counter with a smiling shopkeeper behind it who would sit you on a chair, show you all the goods, help you choose, take your money and count the change into your hand. For our shop, we would select a flat-topped rock for the counter and would spend a happy morning making little sand cakes, and sweets from lumps of clay that crumbled from the cliffs, decorating them with minute pieces of seaweed and tiny shells. We invented our own currency (very handy!) and collected pebbles to be the 'money'. When the tide came in, all our beautiful handiwork was swept away, but that was of no consequence; all the fun had been in the planning and preparation.

The modern child is provided with a ready-made shop, complete with a perfect plastic replica of a cash till filled with plastic coins. The result of all this adult commercial care can be that the children may have the inventiveness removed from their play, and consequently a modern game of 'shops' can be over in a jiffy, whereas my friend and I were happily employed for the whole morning. I have a sneaking suspicion that the more sophisticated modern child (given the chance, and at the right age and stage,) would still love to play as we did. Not many

96

people are fortunate enough to live by a sandy beach, but perhaps an indoor game of 'shops', as played by my own children and their friends, might be as popular now as it was then. There is only one way to find out. Try it!

This is how the game was played. The children would choose to be either shopkeepers or shoppers. The shopkeepers would set out their goods on the coffee table, and price all the items by writing out the tickets or using the number stamps from the printing set. Usually the shop was stocked with an assortment of toys and books but, after Christmas, all the cards took on a new lease of life and were resold at bargain prices. They were arranged tastefully in the 'shop', big ones at the back.

While the shop was being set up, the shoppers made themselves a supply of money. (How useful!) Coins were placed under a sheet of paper and scribbled over with a brown or silver wax crayon. If this was done carefully, the image of the coin would appear clearly on the surface of the paper, and could be cut out. (Making double-sided coins was considered an unnecessary waste of time!) The 'coins' were put in purses, often these were just old envelopes, and, armed with carrier bags, the shoppers visited the shop. During play, animated conversations took place, and things could get quite heated if two children fancied the same article — just like the January Sales!

The game was even more enjoyable when someone had the bright idea of using the dressing-up clothes. It is surprising how much your personality can blossom, given a pair of high-heeled shoes, an exotic hat, a worn-out handbag and an old curtain to wear as a shawl.

Build a Village

Quick

The Toy Library Staff,
The Wolfson Centre,
and R.L.

Kevin had a problem. He had brittle bones, and consequently spent much of his life in his special battery-powered chair. This gave him mobility, but when it came to a question of toys, his choice was quite limited. Anything large or heavy would not do. His local Toy Library did its best, but most of the other members of Kevin's age needed hefty, strong toys. We became modestly skilled at making Origami paper toys and other ephemeral novelties until the happy day when we hit the jackpot and came up with an idea which was perfect for him. The toy we invented could be good play value for any child with nimble, but not strong hands, who would welcome a 'low effort' toy for amusement and variety.

An Occupational Therapist gave me some off-cuts of Plastozote. This is a very light, strong plastic material about 20 mm thick, with small holes all over it. It is normally heated and moulded to make supports and splints. Without the heat treatment, it remains flat and almost weightless. The little holes all over it ask to have something poked in them! With patience, it is possible to colour Plastozote with acrylic paint. It takes several coats to get a really bright colour but, once applied, it is very difficult to remove.

The largest off-cut was chosen and trimmed to a neat shape. It was to form the base of a layout. Roads, green areas, ponds and rivers were painted onto it. Tiny houses and cottages, a hospital, a school, a church, cars, buses, lorries, plenty of trees and some boats were made out of stiff paper. The paper was folded over, and each shape was cut out double. A matchstick was glued between the two layers of paper which provided each shape with a stalk to stick in one of the little holes in the Plastozote. The first shapes were coloured with felt pens, but later models were painted with acrylic. This gave them extra stiffness and a good bold colour.

The construction of this toy took three evenings, but the hours of pleasure it afforded Kevin were well worth the time spent. He had a wonderful time arranging all the tiny pieces to his satisfaction, trying them out in different positions, and imagining the daily life of the communities he created. The bus came to collect the children who lived in the house by the pond and took them to school. Mr Smith drove to the office and a police car chased a baddie! With luck, Kevin will be inspired to add more items to his layout and his play will become even more creative and imaginative.

Materials
- A friendly Occupational Therapist to supply the off-cut of Plastozote!
- Stiff paper and matchsticks for the models

- Acrylic paint for the layout; felt pens will do for the models
- A container for all the small pieces

A Pipe Cleaner Doll on a Button

Quick

R.L.

Here is an idea for a versatile free-standing doll. It can be used to add life to a road or railway layout (perhaps a lollipop lady controlling the crossing or a latecomer running for the train?), or it can be moved around the various rooms in a doll's house. It can even be used as a counter on board games if the squares are large enough. This doll can be an improvement on a bought standing figure. It has greater stability, which enables children with poor hand control to move it around more easily.

To make it, all you need are two pipe cleaners, a large button and some tiny scraps of material for the clothes. If you are new to the art of creating pipe cleaner dolls, first have a look at the one described by Pam Rigley on p. 52. This one is similar, but instead of feet, it will stand on a large button – the kind often used on raincoats, which has its holes recessed and a lip around the edge. To make the legs and body, bend one pipe cleaner in half and poke the ends through the button. Pull it through tightly so that the bend lies within the lip of the button and it will stand flat. (If it doesn't, find another button!) To make the head and arms, fold the other pipe cleaner in half over your little finger. Twist to form the neck and bend the ends to make arms of a suitable length. Hook the tops of the legs over the shoulders (like braces) and twist to form the body. Beware of making the doll too tall, and therefore top heavy. Sometimes, the holes in the button can be too large to grip the pipe cleaner snugly. It will need fixing in place with a dab of UHU. If you want to make a pretty and long-lasting doll to be treasured, fill out the head with a scrap of padding and cover it with a tiny piece of material from an old pair of tights. Embroider the features and add wool hair. Clothes can be made from oddments of ribbon, lace or felt. If you find this too fiddly, just bind the figure with wool. Use a needle to make it easier to wrap around the legs.

MORE PLAY HELPS

See also
Dolls, pp. 50–54
Instant Hats, pp. 77–78
Recipes for Play Pastry, p. 92

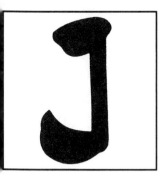

JIGSAWS

How to Enliven a Blank Patch in the Day with Some Instant Jigsaws

Instant

Freda Kim,
Lekotek Korea,
The Toy Library,
Seoul

From the newsletter of Lekotek Korea comes an excellent suggestion for using the strong cardboard boxes that package some toys, and recycling them to make a simple jigsaw. The boxes display a colourful illustration of the toy inside. This will be a familiar plaything to the child, so he can recognise its shape in the picture and should be able to complete the puzzle once he has understood the idea. All you have to do is to trim the illustration to your liking, then cut it into a few bold pieces for the child to fit together again.

Another idea is to use a fairly stiff Christmas card, and stick the front to the back, smearing the glue *all over* an inside surface. When the glue is dry, cut out the card, (now double thickness,) into the required number of shapes.

Neither of these puzzles will stand up to much wear, but perhaps that is part of their attraction. At the end of playtime, they can be disposed of and, if they have been voted a success, a fresh supply can be made on another occasion.

The Puzzle Game

Quick

R.L.

When our family was young and birthday parties were a regular festivity, this game was often used as a 'starter'. It kept the guests busy and happy until everyone had arrived and the fun could begin in earnest. It needed a little advance preparation, but always got the party off to a happy start. Plenty of Christmas cards were cut into pieces. When the children were little, they were just divided in half. One piece of each card was kept in a paper bag, and the other piece was hidden somewhere in the room. The children took a piece from the bag and then had to search around to find the rest of the picture.

Every time a card was completed, the child received a tiny sweet from the box of Dolly Mixture to help him keep his strength up for the next search!

A Feely Doll Inset Puzzle

Long-lasting

Marie Johnson,
Helper,
Kingston-upon-Thames Toy
    Library

A four-year-old partially sighted member of the toy library came in one day and was found rummaging among all the feely toys for something that would take her fancy. She had a problem! As a long-standing toy library member she had gone through the entire stock and was adept at matching texture to texture – the skill required in all games of tactile dominoes and feely Bingo. She wanted something *different* and, frankly, less boring! She liked toys with textural clues, because she could play with them without needing all the paraphernalia of special lenses and lighting.

Marie came up with the splendid idea of making her a feely doll inset puzzle where matching the textures would help her to fit the pieces of puzzle into the correct places. The toy library electric fretsaw was put to work, and by the time our faithful little member made her next visit, the puzzle was created.

A basic shape of a lady (as seen on the doors of toilets) was cut from plywood. The outside shape was mounted on hardboard to make the tray. The head, legs and shoes were cut away from the body and painted. The trunk and skirt were separated from each other and divided down the middle. The two trunk pieces had a velvet surface glued to them to make a luxurious blouse, and the skirt pieces were covered in corduroy. A strong adhesive was used to prevent the fabric from lifting at the edges. The puzzle now consisted of a head, two trunk pieces, two skirt pieces and two legs, part painted, part textured. I am happy to say the puzzle met with complete approval! Because of the confidence it gave her, the little girl started to enjoy other tray puzzles (without textural clues) and learnt to be quick at recognising the outlines of the shapes and holes. With this new-found skill, a whole new cupboard full of puzzles awaited her.

Materials
- Plywood for the puzzle
- Hardboard for the backing
- Paints and textures for the decoration

Matchbox Puzzles from South America

Quick

Nylse de Cunha,
Brazil

Nylse is a teacher of children with special needs, and organises the Brazilian Association of Toy Libraries. She has the enviable skill of being able to create really useful 'teaching' toys from cheap and easily available materials. Her lovely matchbox puzzles prove the point!

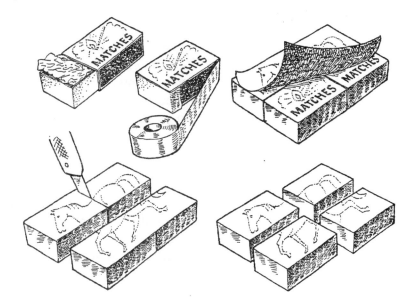

These puzzles are particularly suitable for children who cannot manage to handle the pieces of an ordinary jigsaw, also for those who use their feet instead of their hands. Collect four matchboxes, push them together, face down, and choose two pictures to paste over them. Hold the matchboxes together with masking tape while you stick on the first picture. When the glue is dry, separate the matchboxes with a craft knife, and repeat the process with the second picture. For extra strength, you can stuff each box with a tissue and wrap insulating tape (used by electricians) round the edges. This prevents the children from opening the boxes and safely covers the abrasive sides.

I have tried out this idea and can vouch for its popularity. I used four boxes and grouped them as in the illustration. On one side I pasted a horse and on the reverse side I stuck a picture of a tall giraffe. This meant the boxes had to be arranged a different way to complete each puzzle. The children needed to look extra carefully at the picture to see how the parts joined up.

The matchbox puzzle had its greatest moment of glory when it was successfully put together by a little girl with cerebral palsy. The most controllable part of her body was her head. With the help of her 'Unicorn' head pointer and a baking tray fixed to the table with Blu-tack, she was able to push the chunky boxes against the top edge of the tray and then slide them into the corner in the right order to complete the picture.

Should you decide to copy this idea, you will probably make your own adaptations. For instance, you will need eight boxes if you want to mount a picture that is the size of an illustration from a Ladybird book.

Materials
- Empty matchboxes – four or more; (if necessary extra *weight* in the shape of plasticine or small pebbles can be added for more stability).
- Suitable pictures.
- Glue.
- Tissues (to stuff the boxes for extra strength).
- Electricians' tape (to keep the boxes shut and cover the abrasive sides).
- Optional masking tape (to hold the boxes in position while the pictures are applied).

Push Together Puzzles

Quick

Imagine you have mounted a picture on plywood and have divided it into two by cutting a wavy line down the middle. Before you is the simplest possible push-together puzzle. If you are fortunate enough to have the use of a band saw or an electric jig saw, you are in a position to make these puzzles by the dozen. Each picture can be cut into as many pieces as appropriate for the child in question just by making more wiggly lines.

For all children, this kind of puzzle can form a bridge between inset tray puzzles and ones with interlocking pieces. They are specially suitable for children with very poor hand control because the shapes do not have to be lifted, but are simply pushed together. They have been used successfully by children using a Unicorn head pointer and even by one child who used her feet instead of hands. For such special needs, the pieces need to be confined on a tray with a lip — a biscuit baking tray anchored to the table with Sticky Fixers, Blue-tack etc. is a good choice. The child can push the first piece of the picture into a corner, and then line up all the other pieces alongside it — first arranging them the right way up and in the right order. When using a baking tray as a working surface, it may be helpful to apply small pieces of magnetic tape to the backs of the puzzle pieces. This slows down the sliding action and makes it easier to line up the pieces accurately.

Alternative ways of removing and replacing the pieces of inset puzzles

In answer to the pleas of toy librarians, some manufacturers have introduced into their range inset tray puzzles fitted with large knobs. There is now a good choice available (*see* Educational Suppliers, p. 187). But however hard the toy industry tries to help, it cannot be expected to meet the needs of every child. Often, a small adaptation made to a commercial puzzle may be all that is necessary to turn a session of frustration into one of achievement. If large knobs fitted to the pieces are not the answer for your child, here are four other suggestions which may help.

1. *Raise up the inserted piece.* Cut out an identical piece in plywood or thick card and stick it to the bottom of the original piece. This will now stand proud of the tray and can be handled by grasping it round the edges.

2. *Screw a plasticised curved cup hook into the inset piece.* If the tip protrudes through to the underside, file it flat and smooth. This idea dates from the early days of toy libraries when Audrey Stephenson, an eminent and ingenious toy designer, found that by using this simple device some children with severe cerebral palsy could manage to hook out the pieces and replace them correctly. Being slender, the cup hooks hardly obscure the picture — as often happens when large knobs are attached.

3. *Use a golf tee.* This also makes a fairly unobtrusive knob. It stands out from the inset piece and can be a

suitable shape and size for the child to grip easily. Drill a hole right through the inset piece. If you use a plastic tee, countersink a small depression on the underside of the hole. Poke the tee through the hole so that the point protrudes. Rub this with a hot metal object. This will melt the plastic, causing it to run into the countersunk hole, fusing the tee firmly in place. For this operation, you can use an old spoon heated over the gas stove. To protect your hand, wrap a cloth round the handle, for this will also get hot. If you use a wooden tee, there is no need to countersink. Push the tee in place and smooth off the tip. Pull it out of the hole and apply wood glue, or other strong adhesive, before fixing it finally in place.

4. *Pull out the inset piece with a magnet.* This idea has a strong appeal for children. They seem to see it as some form of magic. It is really very simple. A steel drawing pin is pushed into the inset piece, and a round magnet is glued to a handle using a suitable, strong adhesive. Place the magnet on the pin, and out comes the piece! For children who cannot manage a handle, the magnet can be sewn to a fabric strap with a Velcro fastening. The strap can be worn as a bracelet, or over the child's hand (like a benign knuckle duster!) and by dabbing the magnet on the drawing pin the child can control the placing of the inset piece.

KICKING

KITCHEN PLAY

KICKING

Small babies at nappy-changing time love to scrabble their heels on the plastic sheet. Their pleasure is even greater if some tissue paper – perhaps a piece used to wrap a loaf from the baker – covers the plastic, and even more vigorous kicking will result. At this lying-down stage, cot toys can be stretched across the bars and hung in the right place for kicking. Judy Denziloe's bunch of rattles, or Fiona Priest's balloon with a few grains of rice inside make splendid targets, and they can also be held at the right angle to encourage children in wheelchairs to kick. What about the children who are able to walk, but have difficulty in standing on one leg while they concentrate on kicking with the other? Playing 'Goal Keeper' can make a good game for them. The child stands in a doorway (with the door wedged open, so that there is no danger of it closing on his fingers.) He supports himself by pressing against the door frame, and can then kick out with confidence.

Children who are good at balancing like to play the games suggested by Brian Spencer, Remedial Gymnast, The Manor Hospital. A ball can be kicked between two children to and fro through the legs of a chair, or the legs of a third child. As skill increases, they can stand further apart. For the really skilful, a ball can be dribbled between a row of objects, slalom fashion.

Children in Japan play a game in which a small ball, rather like a round beanbag, must be kept airborne by tossing it for as long as possible with the foot. Oversize

107

shuttlecocks can be bought at sports shops and these may be used to play a modified version of the Japanese game.

See also
   A Large Light Noisy Ball, p. 27
   Pop-up Box, p. 61

KITCHEN PLAY

I guess that ever since saucepans were invented, toddlers have been busy taking them out of the cupboard, putting things in them, fitting the lids correctly and thumping them with a wooden spoon. In the process of collecting the material for this book, many people have given me suggestions for 'kitchen' toys that are easy to make. Often several people have come up with the same ideas, which would indicate their popularity with the children. Here is a list for you to glance through. Perhaps there is something that could appeal to your child; always bearing the safety factor in mind.

- Make a delicate rattle with two foil jam tart cases. Put a few dried peas in one, and cover it with the other. Join them together with Sellotape.

- A sloshy rattle which is also fun to look at can be made by putting a little coloured water into a clear plastic bottle and adding a small quantity of cooking oil. Shake it about, then hold it still and watch the contents separate out. A smear of UHU round the lid should prevent it from being unscrewed accidentally. Alternatively, a few drops of bubble bath can be added to the water. An energetic shake will produce lots of bubbles, and when the bottle is still, these will gradually disappear. Another idea is to add a little oatmeal to the water. This will create a rather grubby snowstorm when shaken. Glitter gives a more spectacular effect!

- Make one of Loet Vos' Instant Dolls (p. 50) using a J cloth.

- Next time you buy a net bag full of nuts, remove a few for the fruit bowl, but leave some to rattle about in the bag. Tie up the opening and use as a feely bag.

- The net bags that contain onions etc. can be turned into instant feely bags by stuffing them with a few milk bottle tops, a scrunched-up paper bag, a foil tart case, a coloured plastic lid from a bottle . . . what ever comes to hand!

- Make some play pastry, recipes on p. 92, and press some into one half of a round cheese portion box. (Use the other half to make a 'Mobile within a Mobile', p. 119.) Poke various shapes into the play pastry to make a collage decoration. Pasta shells, short lengths of drinking straws, bottle tops, a few dried peas or butter beans and any other small handy objects can all be used to good effect. When the pastry has dried out, the ornament can rest on the shelf for all to admire. Older children like to model the play pastry into convincing 'sausages, peas and chips' as food for their dolls and teddies.

- Macaroni can be threaded to make a necklace. String with a little Sellotape wound round one end to stiffen it makes a suitable threader.

- On a hot day, playing with a bowl of water which has a few ice cubes bobbing about in it has its attractions. They can be stirred around to chink against the sides of the bowl, or briefly held and then put on one side, so that they can be observed disintegrating into a puddle.
- Put something into a jumbo matchbox and invite your child to work out how to open it and find the surprise.
- Blow up a paper bag and pop it. Not for those of a nervous disposition, but immensely popular with the hard of hearing!
- Cake tins can be used for stacking or nesting, and bun tins with their individual compartments make excellent sorting trays.
- The peg bag also has possibilities for play. The pegs can be pinched into the lip of a tin or cardboard box to make a fence round the top, or they can be clipped together in a long line to make a snake or alligator.
- If you want to use cooking essences like vanilla or peppermint to make a smelly toy, dilute the essence by adding a few drops of cooking oil. Neat peppermint, for instance, can be quite painful to smell, if you do not approach it delicately!
- Try finger painting, using a mixture of cornflour and water. Mix these together to make a fairly stiff dough — only a very little water is needed. Put the mixture on a Formica-topped table and watch it spread out. It can be collected up and dribbled through the fingers to make even more amazing shapes! It is shiny and has an attractive feel. It is also easy to clear up! Any spills on the carpet can be vacuumed up when they are dry.
- *Real* participation in the life of the kitchen is the best part of all — especially when this includes helping with the cooking, even at the most basic level, perhaps breaking up the spaghetti for the Bolognaise or scraping out the cool custard saucepan!

See also
Playing at the Sink, p. 175
Sorting in an Egg Box, p. 178

LISTENING

A Loopy Rattle

Quick

Alison Wisbeach,
Head Occupational Therapist,
The Wolfson Centre,
and R.L.

A small light-weight rattle was needed for a baby with very tiny hands. Alison thought up the idea of making one from a golf practice ball, which is plastic, very light, and covered with convenient holes. Three short lengths of clear polythene tubing could be poked in and out of the holes, and the ends of each piece joined together to make a loop. The join could be heat sealed by melting the plastic on one end of the tube and holding it against the opposite end until it cooled and fused together. Before doing all this technical stuff, a few tiny beads were put in one potential loop and a drop of coloured water in another. The third was left plain. By slightly vandalising the golf practice ball, it was possible to push a small bell inside. This was tied in place to prevent it from escaping through the enlarged hole. I am happy to report that this strange loopy rattle was perfect for the child to hold. Waving it about to jingle the bell, and watching the contents of the loops slop about inside the tubes gave her much pleasure.

A Strong Rattle

Instant

Christine Cousins,
Educational Psychologist

It is not easy to find a diversion for a child who may not only have difficulty in grasping her toys, but also has a sight or hearing loss. Perhaps the rattle in a plastic container which Christine has devised may help. To make it, you need a plastic bottle with a built-in handle, such as one used for fabric softener. Into this put two large metal nuts. Smear some UHU adhesive to the neck of the bottle before firmly screwing on the lid. Wait a little while for the glue to set, and the rattle is ready for play. The handle of the bottle is easy to grasp, and, in use, the rattling metal can be felt as well as heard. All these attributes make it suitable for many children who have outgrown or become bored with other smaller rattles.

Jumbo Shaker

Quick

Made by Rosemary
   Hemmett when she was
   Toy Librarian at St Ebba's
   Hospital

Do you ever search in vain for a really large rattle which is sufficiently strong to be used by an older child for whom 'baby' rattles are too small and fragile, and definitely not 'age appropriate'? Perhaps Rosemary's suggestion is just what you need.

She uses a salad shaker – the sort that looks like two plastic collanders joined together with a hinge. Normally, the freshly washed lettuce is put between the halves, and rapidly shaken to remove all the surplus water. Replace the lettuce with a few ping-pong balls (coloured for choice) or better still some cat balls from the pet shop. These are made of coloured plastic, and have small bells inside. Tie the two halves of the salad shaker together, bind round the handle so that the two parts cannot be separated, and you will have a very strong, large rattle which can be carried around or hung up to be biffed or kicked. I have made several of these over the years and can vouch for their durability and popularity.

Some Unusual Noisemakers

All Instant or Quick

A peripatetic teacher discovered that the most attractive noisemaker for one of her little pupils was a large comb that could be drawn across the bars of a metal radiator! The comb was attached to the pipes by a length of elastic so that the child, who was visually handicapped, always knew where to find it. It seems to me there is a moral in this discovery. So often we present children with nice tidy shop-bought rattles which sometimes meet with a luke-warm reception. Something really 'Off Beat' can have far more child appeal!

Another example is the unusual noisemaker accidentally discovered by a three-year-old. She had finished eating the contents of a plastic pot, and noticed it had a ridged pattern round the edge of the bottom. She soon realised that drawing her spoon over these ridges made a loud and distinctive sound capable of stopping the mealtime conversation! (A child who finds it difficult to grasp a spoon in one hand and a pot in the other could practise the skill by playing the 'pot and spoon' in the band!)

Children who have very poor hand function may be unable to join in the music session with much enjoyment simply because there are so few instruments they can control. Here are a few suggestions which may help to give them more choice.

1. *Make bell bracelets* by attaching bells (obtainable at pet shops) to a strip of material. Join this into a circle by sewing a strip of Velcro to each end. It can then be attached comfortably to whatever part of the child's body he finds easiest to control, e.g. wrist, ankle, knee or forehead. You can also use a sweat band.

2. *Hang a tambourine* within easy reach, so that it can be biffed as required. Make sure it is secured at three points, so that it will not twist or swing.

3. *Make sand blocks* for a child who can only use one hand by fixing a piece of sandpaper to the table with masking tape. Then cover a block of wood with more sandpaper and the child can rub this on the sheet with his able hand.

If holding a drum and stick is not possible for a child who would dearly like to play such a prestigious instrument, try stretching a loop of elastic over the head of the drum. This will need anchoring down with a piece of string tied round the outside of the drum, so that you end up with two taut strands of elastic across the head. The child can pluck these and let them slap back on the drum head as the music dictates. It requires a great deal of concentration and skill to play *one* drum beat at the appropriate moment, e.g. when the clock strikes in Hickery Dickery Dock. The thrill of getting it right is well worth the agonising suspense!

Ideas contributed by Stephanie Clements' little daughter, Christine Cousins, John Gould and teachers of children with cerebral palsy.

Find the Pairs

Quick

Margaret Gilman, Teacher,
White Lodge Spastics Centre

In the nursery class at White Lodge, the children enjoy their daily drinks of Nesquik. By the end of the term a useful collection of empty tins has been saved. Margaret uses these to make a sound-matching game suitable for the children in her care. Pairs of tins are given a small amount of the same contents — rice, pebbles, bells, buttons etc. Because of their size and shape, the children are able to shake the tins and stand them up in pairs when they have found two that make the same sound.

See also

A Musical Half Moon, p. 119
An Echo Blaster Windmill Dice, p. 122

MOBILES

In the beginning of history I guess little cave babies lying on their sabre-toothed tiger skin rugs, gurgled with delight as they watched the leaves on the trees rustle in the breeze and the clouds drift across the mouth of the cave. Watching a gently moving object can be both soothing and diverting, which is why tanks of tropical fish are so popular in medical waiting rooms.

Think of a modern tiny baby lying in his cot, unable to lift or turn his head to get a view of what lies outside the bars. The only thing he has to look at is the blank ceiling above. It is possible for this situation to continue to be part of the daily life of older children, who are unable to move independently and have to stay where they are put. Such total dependence can also be temporary, when illness or injury forces a child to stay in one place. Under these circumstances, a colourful and interesting mobile can certainly help to relieve the monotony.

There are mobiles of every description in the shops. Some clamp to a cot-side and play a tune while gently rotating, others are made in brilliant colours and are made to be hung up so that they will slowly move in the draught. There are even mobiles for the desk tops of harrassed top executives. Delightful as these manufactured mobiles can be, they have their limitations, e.g. some are too small for the children to see easily. Moreover, there is a need for frequent change if the child's interest is to be held, and if only bought mobiles are used this can lead to considerable expense. How much more satisfactory to create your own, preferably with the help of the family.

No extravagant claims are made for the originality of some of the ideas that follow. Some are 'old hat' to many teachers, but may not be to the children. All are easy to make, often only needing some felt pens and thin card for their construction. Perhaps you will make your version extra large, or will include some shiny paper or coloured cellophane to liven it up. Maybe it will jingle or rustle as it moves in the draught. Something suggested in this section may give you ideas of your own. Of one thing you can be sure. Because you have *thought* about it, your special mobile will be just right for the child in question.

Why not turn off the telly, gather the family round the kitchen table, and have a go!

A Variety of Mobiles from the Rix Toy Library

Quick

Monica Taylor,
Toy Librarian

I visited the Rix Toy Library at the Normansfield Hospital shortly before Christmas. This was an ideal time, for the workroom was strewn with mobiles ready to hang in the wards and units. The residents had helped to make many of these and must have enjoyed themselves producing such colourful and interesting results. Three of the more popular designs are described below.

A Snowman Mobile

Cut two snowman shapes from thin card. Decorate both sides of each piece. (Face, hat, scarf, broom, pipe.) Make a slit in one piece from the middle of the *top* to the centre, and in the other from the middle of the *bottom* to the centre. The two pieces will now interlock, giving you a snowman who faces North, South, East and West!

The same principle of interlocking two identical shapes can also be applied to Christmas trees, stars, etc. – in fact to any symmetrical shape.

The Disco Window

This is a circular shape with transparent coloured spots. Begin with two circles of card, which is stiff enough to hold its shape and does not go floppy, and make the circles about the size of a dinner plate. In each, cut out several identical small holes. Make sure that when the two large circles are put together, the holes match up and you can see through them. Colour the outsides of both cards. Take one card, and on the inside cover all the small holes with coloured cellophane (sweet wrappings will do). Stick the other card on top. Hang near the

116

window, so that the sun will shine through the holes and make patterns on the wall or floor.

A Mobile Like a Humming Top (without the hum!)

This one is made from two shallow cones joined together, giving them the shape of a humming top. In this case, one end points to the ceiling and the other to the floor. Start with two identical circles of card, (use the dinner plate again) and decorate them. Now picture them as a round cake and cut yourself a stingy slice! This small wedge shape must be removed from both circles. Overlap the cut edges and stick them together. Fix a hanging thread to one. The best way is to tie a button to the end of the thread to prevent it from pulling out, then poke the other end up through the centre of the shape. Stick or staple the two halves together.

Optional Extra. Before the halves are joined together, short narrow tissue paper streamers can be stuck to the inside of the lower shape. These make an attractive fringe and will rustle in the draught.

Shiny Mobiles

A mobile which will catch the light, and therefore may appeal to a child with partial sight, can be simply made by hanging up interesting shiny shapes like a baby mirror, strings of milk bottle tops, small boxes wrapped in foil paper, or a tin lid, decorated perhaps on one side with a pattern using Humbrol Enamel.

For *an extra large shiny mobile* suitable for a big room, Jean Vant from Australia suggests hanging up the silver container from a wine box. Inflate it, and perhaps add some paper streamers to flutter in the breeze.

To make *a rustly mobile* use two paper plates. These are ultimately joined together to make a flat cushion. Make several strings of milk bottle tops, first putting a button on the end of the string to stop them from slipping off. Attach the strings to the edge of the lower plate. Insert the hanging thread into the centre of the top plate – remember the button on the bottom of this too – and staple the plates together.

Angela Sanches from the Thomas Coram Childrens' Centre has made a *glittering mobile* by cutting delicate butterfly shapes from sequin scrap – the part that is left behind after the machine has punched out all the sequins. The holes give the butterflies a frail, ethereal look. Pipe cleaners, folded in half, are used to make the bodies and antennae.

A Bird Mobile

Quick

Bedelsford School

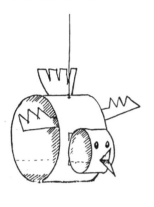

A flock of these attractive birds hangs in the corner of the classroom where the children take their daily rest. They are made entirely in white paper with only their orange beaks and large black eyes to add a touch of colour. The effect is gentle and soothing. Just right for rest time!

The body of each bird is made from a ring of paper (like a napkin ring) and the head is made from a smaller ring. Once these are stuck together, your imagination can take over and you can complete your bird as you wish. A beak can be made by cutting out a diamond-shaped piece of paper, folding it in half, and sticking it to the head. Mark in the eyes with felt pen. If you want wings, cut both out together and stick them to the inside of the body ring. (The birds at Bedelsford School are wingless, and look quite convincing! They remind me of baby chicks.) You can make a drooping tail or one that sweeps upwards, according to the way you attach it to the body.

A Shoal of Fish

Quick

Bedelsford School

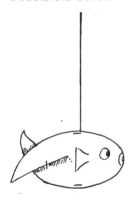

When they are finished, these fish have a chubby, three dimensional look. To make them, cut out two identical oval-shaped pieces of stiff paper. While they are still flat, decorate them as you wish. You might like to make each side different — some fish are like that! One half could be coloured and the other covered with foil paper. This gives a striking effect when the fish are finally revolving gently at the ends of their strings. Sequins make excellent fishes' eyes.

In each fish shape, cut a horizontal slit from the tail end to about the middle of the body. Take the two parts of the tail and make them overlap so the points stick out beyond the body. Stick or staple them together. The body now bows outwards and this slightly domed shape will give the fish its final 3D effect. If you would like your fish to have fins at the top and bottom of his body, fix these in place before you join the two sides together (glue or staple). If the fish tends to collapse on you at this stage, and lose his nice fat shape, put a scrunched-up tissue inside him to pad him out. Add the side fins.

To find the best position for the hanging thread, poke a

needle through the body at the place where you think it should go, and see how the fish balances. All do not have to swim straight. The mobile looks more interesting if a few fish with independent spirits head for the surface of the water, and others for the sandy bottom!

A Mobile Within a Mobile

Quick

Susie Mason,
Toy Librarian,
The Thomas Coram Centre

Susie has a delightfully simple way of creating a mobile in which the centre part moves independently from the outside. She starts with a round cheese box and removes the cardboard centre. This leaves the rim to make the frame, which is painted in a bright colour. From the discarded cardboard she makes an interesting shape – a face, an animal, a boat, a flower, a Christmas tree . . . the possibilities are endless! This shape is coloured on both sides and suspended in the centre of the circular frame. When both parts are hung up, each can rotate independently from the other.

Circular Mobiles a Child Can Sit Inside

Quick

To make one of these, you need a large plastic hoop and some means of hanging it horizontally from at least three points, and at the right height for it to encircle the child's head like an outsize halo. The idea is to surround the child with large colourful objects he can biff at, and so make the mobile *mobile*! There are several ways of decorating the hoop. Use several balloons for a spectacular effect, but the strings should not be too long or they tend to tangle.

At Linden Bennet School, the teachers hang cardboard tubes from the insides of rolls of baking foil, kitchen towel etc., covered with foil paper or paint.

At White Lodge Spastics Centre, Margaret Gilman favours a noisy version. Her hoop is bedizened with tin lids (no sharp edges), so that when a child activates them, they jangle together.

A Musical Half Moon
(weather resistant)

Long-lasting

Ida Codrington, Student,
Toy Making Course, London
College of Furniture

Most mobiles are hung out of reach for they are intended only to be looked at. This one is different. It is shaped like a crescent moon (cut out of plywood) and about ten short lengths of bamboo dangle from the lower edge. Knock these together and you produce a delightful noise and a changing pattern of lines. Because it is made from wood, this mobile is very tough, and is best hung *within reach* of the children, so they can stretch up and set the bamboo pieces all a-jingle. It can also be hung outside as a wind chime, and will come to no harm in the rain. I can imagine it outside a window, hanging from the bare branches of a tree, and making a welcome splash of colour in a dreary winter landscape.

A dinner plate would make a suitable template for marking the outside edge of the moon. A small hole for the hanging thread is drilled near the upper point and several more holes, for the bamboo, are made around the lower edge. They need to be suitably spaced out so the hanging pieces do not touch each other when 'at rest', but knock together to make a pleasing noise when the moon is moved.

The pieces of bamboo are cut from garden cane. Making them different lengths and thicknesses will vary the sounds they produce. Saw the cane into pieces, making each cut about 10 mm above each joint. Prepare each piece of cane by cleaning out the pith from the middle (use thin dowel or a knitting needle). Drill a small hole through the joint for the hanging thread. Poke this through the hole and out of the bottom of the bamboo. Tie a *large* knot, and pull the thread back up so that the knot rests below the joint, ready for hanging. Scrape all the waxy coat from the outside of the bamboo (use a penknife and sandpaper). Paint all the pieces and when dry add a coat (or two!) of Polyurethane varnish for extra protection. Finally, attach the lengths of bamboo to the holes in the lower edge of the moon, hang it in a suitable place – and wait for the compliments to pour in!

How to hang up your mobile

The choice is wide. It is just a question of finding the best method for *you*. Here are some suggestions.

At the Wolfson Centre, in a corridor where the ceiling is fairly low, you will see tiny paper mobiles hanging from crossed drinking straws. If you had attended the twentieth birthday party of the Kingston Toy Library, you would have found the large hall decorated with rows of upturned umbrellas, their frames dripping with enormous toy and animal shapes made by the local secondary school.

In between these two extremes are many alternatives. Some people use an ordinary wire coathanger and tie their shapes to the bottom rail. Others go one step further and use two coathangers, removing one hook, interlocking them and taping them together so they form a cross. The shapes can be hung from all four points. A lampshade frame is another useful ready-made hanger. It needs to be suspended from three points to make it hang level.

Where a large mobile is needed, say in a schoolroom or a hall, some people use a garden cane or a plastic hoop. There is also the old umbrella mentioned above. If you choose this method, cut away most of the cover, just leaving a narrow border round the edge. This acts as a spacer, and keeps the ribs evenly apart. Any broken spines must be taped together. (As the umbrella is heavier than all the other suggestions, make sure it is securely attached to its fitting, and there is no danger of it falling down.)

If you want to hang your mobile like the commercial ones, with a series of horizontal wire rods dangling from each other and a shape attached to each end, a useful tip is to start with the bottom pair first, and work upwards. Tying the mobile together this way, makes it easier to adjust the balance as you go. When all is correct and each arm of the mobile is hanging level and can rotate without touching another, fix the strings in place with a blob of UHU.

The best thread to use for paper or card shapes is button thread. This has a twist in it which helps the shapes to rotate.

Where to hang your mobile

A mobile is meant to *move*, so choose a position where it will be in a slight draught, perhaps near a door or window. Consider the position carefully. What might be right for you could be quite wrong for a small child whose eye level is so much nearer the floor. He should *enjoy* looking at the mobile – after all that is the whole purpose of the exercise! – and should be able to see it without strain. Before you tie the final knot, try viewing the mobile from the same angle as the child will see it.

NUMBER

An Echo Blaster Windmill Dice

Long-lasting

Jusuf Raymond,
Student,
Handicap Education and Aids
  Research Unit (HEARU),
City of London Polytechnic

The words 'Echo Blaster' in the title of this toy are most appropriate. The noise it makes when rotated is *very* loud! Jusuf, a student at HEARU, designed it to be easily manipulated by children who have difficulty in using their hands. It can be used as an outsize dice for group games. The figures at the sides, or for visually handicapped children the raised upholstery tacks, indicate the number 'thrown'. It also makes a splendidly noisy table top rattle, which could appeal to a child with a hearing loss.

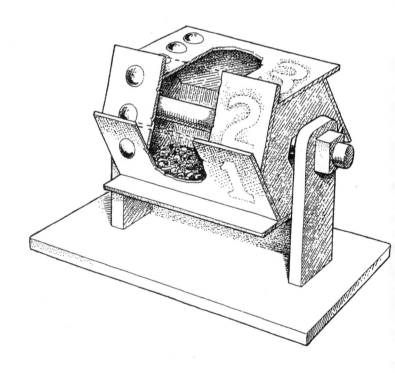

The illustration shows the construction of the dice far better than I can describe it! There is no particularly recommended size, but as a guide, the original sides were about 240 mm wide. The arresting noise is created by a hotch-potch of metal objects which are put into the dice before the final panel is fixed in place. Jusuf used nuts and bolts, washers and a few bells. The large hole for the spindle and the protruding sides make the box easy to turn over, even for children who find it difficult to uncurl their fingers. The large base makes it very stable.

Going on the Bus

Quick

Joanna Sacks,
Playgroup Mum

Joanna has made a simple number game for two children which involves counting from one to three. The game consists of two base boards on which cross sections through two buses are drawn, revealing the empty passenger seats (say eleven of them) and one for the driver. One bus is coloured red and the other blue. Counters represent the passengers and they are allowed to enter or alight from the bus according to the throw of a dice.

Joanna makes her passengers from the plastic screw top lids from 2-litre orange squash containers, the contents having been previously consumed by the playgroup. The lids have a chunky shape which is easy for the children to manipulate. Each one is given a red or blue face to indicate which bus it must catch. The features are made from peel-off plastic shapes – easy to apply, but Joanna confesses they sometimes come adrift. Drawing faces with red and blue marker pens could be better. (Two spots for eyes, and a half moon for a smiling mouth.) The dice is made from an unwanted brick and one, two or three spots are applied in each colour.

To play the game, each child takes charge of a bus, and must first throw a 1 in his colour before the driver can take his seat. After that it is all plain sailing, and every time the correct colour is thrown that number of passengers can join the bus until all the seats are full. But that is not the end of the game. It continues until all the passengers have alighted, the driver being the last to leave. This gives the game a neat twist, for the principles of addition and subtraction are both introduced.

As with all home-made toys, this game can be adapted

to include more children by enlarging the fleet of buses and using two dice.

A Number Scrap-book

Quick

R.L.

When children first learn to count, it can be hard to think up different ways of helping them to realise the meaning of number. It may be easy to learn to count parrot fashion, but it is much more difficult to understand that 'three' means more than 'two'. By using 'three' in as many different ways as possible, the conception of that number may be gradually acquired. Perhaps the child can choose three sweets, count out three pennies, fetch three spoons, or pour out three cups of milk! The reinforcing of the idea of number can be carried still further if the child is presented with a pile of pictures (old Christmas cards come in useful again!) and he is invited to pick out all those with, say, one item on them; one candle, one robin, one choir boy etc. The process can be repeated with two items, and so on. The pictures can be mounted in a scrap-book, all the 'ones' on the first page, then the 'twos' etc.

See also
Shake and Make (for counting up to 6) p. 47

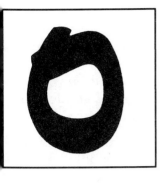

OUTINGS

Two ways of attaching toys to a child

These ideas can be useful for children who like to 'doodle', and for those with busy and sometimes under-occupied hands. On a long journey, the play pinny in particular can be a boon for *any* young child strapped in his car seat, possibly with no one beside him to retrieve lost toys. The tapes used to attach the toys need to be fairly short to prevent them tangling. This can make it difficult for the child to *see* what he is playing with, but a little ingenuity can usually solve the problem!

Play Pinny

Quick

Over the years our toy library at Kingston-upon-Thames has been supplying these pinnies (beautifully made by the home economics class of a local secondary school) to many young visually handicapped or profoundly disabled children.

The basic pattern for a play pinny is just an oblong of material, the width of the child's shoulders, with a hole cut in the middle for his head to go through. A long pocket is made along the bottom of the front. It is divided into two by a row of stitching down the middle to make a separate pocket for each hand. Three loops of tape are sewn to the front of the pinny. It is wise to put a reinforcing strip behind these and to sew them on very securely, for they will have to stand up to much pulling and tweaking. The raw edges are neatened by binding round the neck and making hems at the sides and bottom of the back. Short lengths of tape are stitched to each side. When these are tied together they stop the pinny from rucking up when it is worn. Now all that is needed are some suitable toys to tie to the loops of tape in the front, and to put in the pockets. Rattles, teethers and soft toys are the usual choice.

For a child who dribbles, a waterproof bib can be worn under the pinny to keep his chest dry and comfortable.

Use an Old Belt as a Doodle Holder

Instant

R.L.

Decide on the best place to put the buckle when the belt is round the child's waist. This will probably be at the side of him. Then cut three slots in that part of the belt which will be in the front when it is being worn. Tie a short length of tape to favourite toys and attach them to the belt through the slots.

A slightly more elaborate belt was made for a particular child who had a passion for stroking rough textures. In an effort to broaden his horizons a little, and introduce him to different feels, we used strips of material instead of tape for a background, and stitched buttons to the top of each. They were poked through the slots in the belt, making the strips easily interchangeable. One strip had a nylon pan scrubber firmly attached. On another, pieces of Scotchbrite cleaning pad were chopped up and sewn on in strips, like the rungs of a ladder, and a third had a small nylon nailbrush stitched to it, bristles upwards. Two spare strips were decorated with a row of metal buttons and some hair rollers. Once these items were accepted and 'doodled' with, the idea was developed to include more exciting strips of fabric and a wider variety of objects to feel. These included a bunch of bells, a strip of Velcro to open and close, a stone with a hole in it, and various strong rattles.

A Good Colour Game for Journeys

Quick

Joan Thorpe,
Librarian,
Merry-go-round Toy Library,
Frimley

Make lots of cards with a colour on one side. Each child has a handful of cards, stacked with the coloured side down. The top card is turned over. When something of that colour is spotted, that card is put aside and the next one turned up, and so on through the pile. The object of course is to use up the cards as quickly as possible. As a variation: (a) you can set a time or distance limit; (b) with a group of very observant children who are likely to finish the game too quickly the used cards can be put at the bottom of someone else's pile!

If you are feeling thrifty, the cards can be made from the backs of old Christmas cards cut to roughly the same size. For speed, the colour can be a large spot applied with felt pen.

A Novelty Notebook

Almost Instant

For children who are able to draw or write, a tiny notebook, made from an old Christmas card with a few pages stitched inside and a stump of pencil tied to it, can happily while away a few miles.

Useful travel tips

'Thinking Little' (p. 190) is a mail order firm which specialises in practical and innovative products to make journeys easier for parents and more comfortable for children. They can supply items like car blinds, a soft towelling safety head restraint, a no-strings bib etc.

If you are heading for the sun, a coloured protection cream which can be used like face paints is available from all branches of the Body Shop.

Books worth consulting are:

Games for Journeys
by Deborah Manley and Peta Ree,
published by Piccolo

and

Family Days Out in Britain
(Where to go – what to do)
Obtainable from A.A. offices and large booksellers.

For air and rail travel consult:

Care in the Air
Advice for Handicapped Airline Passengers
Obtainable (free!) from:
Air Transport Users Committee,
129 Kingsway,
London, WC2B 6NN

British Rail and Disabled Travellers
Free leaflet available from all Main Line stations or:
British Railways Board,
Rail House,
Euston Square,
London, NW1 2DZ

MORE PLAY HELPS

See also

POSTING

Posting Acorns in a Bottle

Quick

Susan Myatt,
Parent,
Kingston-upon-Thames Toy
    Library

All children occasionally welcome the chance to desert their toys and play with natural objects and things from the adult world. These are the nuts and bolts of our environment and through them young children learn about the surroundings in which they live. Picture in your mind's eye a two-year-old totally absorbed in fitting the lids on heavy saucepans. A year later splashing in the puddles or scuffing up the autumn leaves, and his big sister playing at 'weddings' by draping herself in an old net curtain and wearing her mother's shoes. For many children, these delights are out of reach, but *if* you are reading this in the autumn, and *if* you live near an oak tree, and *if* your child has just reached the 'posting' stage, when he loves to put one thing inside another, here is a chance to bring the outside world nearer to him and let him practise his new-found skill into the bargain – and all completely free!

You need a bag full of acorns, (perhaps you and your child can collect them together) and a bottle. If you want him to practise fine finger movements, choose a bottle with a neck just wide enough to receive an acorn end on. Now sit back and watch his delight as he sees the bottle gradually filling up because of his own skilful efforts.

Note: If you use a glass bottle, be sure it is put out of reach when you have finished playing with it together.

Posting Drinking Straws in a Bottle

Instant

Lorraine Crawford's
little daughter

This idea is similar to the one above but it has two special advantages. It can be set up in an instant and does not rely on a seasonal supply of acorns.

Lorraine's small daughter was playing on the kitchen floor when an empty milk bottle caught her attention. Here was an unusual container just waiting to be filled!

A Tactile Posting Box

Long-lasting

Rachel Herman,
Hospital Play Specialist

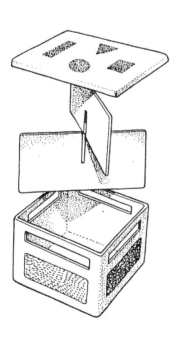

She tried to push her spoon down the neck, but soon discovered that only the handle would fit. In spite of all her efforts, the bowl remained outside. She then searched around for something different to put in the bottle. She had instant success with a pot of pencils, but even better was the bunch of drinking straws someone thoughtfully gave her. These were so long and bendy that she had to line each one up with the neck of the bottle before carefully dropping it in.

Rachel has made an original dual purpose posting box where the shapes are cut from plywood and are covered with distinctive textures. They can either be posted flat, (like posting a letter through a slot,) or they can be grouped together by shape and stacked up on the lid.

The posting box is made from a square plastic food storage container with a lid. A wide slot is cut near the top of each side, and under it an identifying strip of tactile material is glued. A set of shapes is covered with this same material, and the process is repeated for the other three sides and sets of shapes. Now each set can be posted through its own special slot. If you want to check that a child can identify the textures correctly on his own, the box can have dividers inserted to keep the shapes separate. The dividers are made from two pieces of cardboard, cut slightly smaller than the diagonal measurement. Slots are cut halfway across the middle of each so that they will interlock.

To turn the box into a shape-matching activity, each shape is painted on the lid. The individual pieces are sorted into sets of four (one of each *texture*) and matched to their correct position on the lid.

This posting box could be a useful addition to any toy library stock. The use of textures makes it particularly suitable for children with a visual handicap, but the prototype which was used in a hospital ward found favour with all the children at the shapes posting stage. The toy also has two important practical advantages. The shapes are easily replaced if any are lost, and the toy makes its own container so does not need a special bag!

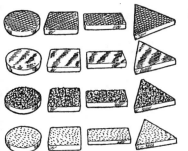

Materials

- A square plastic food container with a lid.
- Plywood or thick cardboard for the shapes.
- Four materials with distinctive textures. (For suggestions, *see* p. 76.)
- Cardboard for the dividers.
- Strong glue, e.g. UHU, Evostick. Be sure to stick the edges down well to deter the 'pickers'!

See also

One Hole Posting Boxes, p. 87
Where Does It Go? p. 150

QUIET ACTIVITIES

A Motor Tyre Sand Pit

Long-lasting

Lena Baum,
Specialist in Play

A photograph sent to me by Lena shows a trio of Israeli boys using a very large tyre sand pit as a ready made den. They are sitting inside with their legs pointing towards the centre and their heads just appearing above the rim, obviously enjoying each other's company and a good chat. There are signs that younger children have occupied the sand pit too. Crumbling sand castles and a few sand toys tell the tale.

The idea of using an old lorry or tractor tyre as a container for sand is one that has many advantages:

- It is cheap – possibly free!
- There are plenty about, if you can find the right place to look.
- It can be scrubbed clean, and even smartened up with a coat of paint.
- It has high sides, which make it an ideal container for the sand.
- It can easily be covered with a plastic sheet,

weighted down to keep out the rain and visiting cats, but best of all . . .

- It can provide some support for a disabled child in need of a back rest.

Why not copy the Israeli boys? The children can sit inside with their backs supported by the tyre rim. They can see and touch each other, play with the sand and have a companionable time together.

Rubbing Boards

Quick

Jean Skinner,
The Manor Hospital Adult
Training Centre

Picture a familiar scene – the rain tumbling down on a depressing afternoon and a room full of bored, fractious children. How satisfactory to be able to produce a wonderful new activity guaranteed to cheer everybody up! Jean's rubbing boards might fill the bill nicely. As this is not an 'instant' activity, it is necessary to prepare it in advance.

The boards are easy to make, but the time-consuming part is collecting all the interesting bits and pieces to make the patterns. These must then be mounted and time must be allowed for the glue to dry.

Each board is made from a piece of stiff cardboard. Various flat items are stuck on to create a raised pattern. To use the boards, cover them with a sheet of paper, rub with a wax crayon and watch the pattern appear. No particular skill is needed, but patience and care will produce a very pleasing result. The principle is one that has been around for a considerable time. Perhaps when you were young, you made money for your 'pretend' shop by putting coins under the paper and rubbing them with a wax crayon, or maybe you rubbed over leaf shapes in your early days at school. Rubbing church brasses is the same activity in a more advanced form.

When you have made a little stock pile of rubbing boards and it is time to use them, anchor each one and its covering paper to the table with Blu-tack, masking tape or Sellotape. The rubbing should be done with the side of the crayon, not the point which may easily poke through the paper. Some children may find it difficult to control a crayon used this way, for there is not much surface to get hold of. It may help to wedge the crayon between the bristles of an old nail brush. Heelball, also known as cobblers' wax, can be used instead of wax crayon. It is very hard and unmessy, and is made in oblong sticks about 150 x 25 x 20 mm. It is obtainable from shoe repairers in black or brown, and craft shops who sell it in silver and gold for brass rubbing. These chunky sticks can be used upright in the usual way, and the broad tip soon rounds into a good surface for rubbing.

Materials

- Pieces of stiff cardboard, say 230 mm square. Any shape will do, providing it is a generous size. This will encourage a free rubbing movement.
- Items to stick on. Here are some suggestions:

  1. Cut out cardboard shapes, arranged at random or in a pattern.
  2. String in a wiggly line.
  3. Flat plastic tea stirrers, arranged in a circle or fan shape.
  4. Keys, buttons, coins, etc., all the same thickness.
  5. Words, names, numbers, made from specially cut-out sandpaper shapes, or pieces of pipe-cleaner.
  6. Textured wallpaper, corrugated cardboard, bubbly plastic.

- Glue – use a strong one.
- Paper – not too thin or it is easily torn and the raised surfaces can poke through; not too stiff or the outlines may be blurred.
- Wax crayons – or heelball.

Footnote. The rubbing boards can also be used to make wax-resistant patterns. Rub the covering paper with an ordinary white domestic candle. Because the white wax does not show up clearly on the paper, it is necessary to work in an orderly fashion, say from top to bottom, or left to right, to make sure all the raised surfaces have been covered properly. Then comes the magic part! Using a thick brush and fairly sloppy paint, quickly cover the paper with a wash of colour. The design on the board underneath should now appear on the paper as a white pattern on a coloured ground.

Cutting activities

'Cutting out' was one of the favourite quiet activities of my childhood. There is something very satisfying about the action of snipping with scissors – the noise perhaps, or the feel. All children seem to enjoy using scissors, but for some the physical act of bringing the blades together is a very difficult one, and possibly they may only be able to make straight snips. It can be hard to think up different ways of using this basic skill, but here are some ideas which may be helpful.

First of all let's consider the scissors. There is a choice of several different types which are available through educational suppliers (e.g. Rompa, Hestair Hope, E. J. Arnold, Peta Scissorcraft, pp. 187–190). Some are designed to be used by the child with an adult hand covering his, and really doing most of the work! This helps the child to learn the opening and closing action required to operate the blades. Perhaps the more popular scissors are the self-opening kind that have had the fingers and thumb rings on the handle replaced by a strip of springy plastic which covers one handle, then curves over to cover the other one, joining them together with a pliable loop. The handles of the scissors are compressed in the normal way, and the loop is flattened. When the child stops squeezing, the handles spring apart, automatically preparing the blades for the next cut. These scissors can also be bought mounted on a block of wood, so that a child who is only able to use one hand can slide the paper between the blades, then press on the loop to close them and make the cut. At the Kingston Toy Library several different types are kept in stock. These can be borrowed in the normal way, and if the child can manage them, most parents like to buy a pair for keeps. Your toy library might also have a range of scissors to try out.

Now comes the fun part. Having just learnt to snip, how can this new skill be used? Here are a few ideas to start you off. Together you might:

- *Make a garden picture.* Your child snips a strip of green paper to make the grass, while you cut out the flowers to grow in it.

- *Make a mosaic picture.* Collect pictures with large areas of one colour from various magazines. Next, draw the outline of a simple shape, like a tree or a flower. Pieces of paper of a suitable colour are snipped from the magazine pictures and pasted, like a mosaic, to fill in the shape.
- *Make a waver.* This consists of lots of long strips of paper which are stuck to the cardboard tube from the inside of a toilet roll. (Use PVA adhesive. It will wash off clothes – and children!) The result, when dry, can be shaken about or waved in time to music in a similar fashion to the huge pom-poms used by cheer leaders at an American ball game!

At a later stage, an out-of-date mail order catalogue can provide hours of fun for children who can cut round corners. The people can be cut out and used as paper dollies, perhaps made into families, or classes of children for playing 'Let's Pretend School'. The furniture and household goods can be used to make a large house poster. A cross-section through a house is drawn, with all the rooms inside visible. These can be furnished appropriately with beds, diningroom furniture, kitchen equipment, a sittingroom, bathroom, etc., and if space permits a garden can surround it, with suitable tools in the shed.

Old Christmas cards can be another source of joy. They can be used to make a counting book (one Christmas tree, two snowmen, three robins, four holly leaves etc.) and, of course, to make a scrap-book. At Moorfields Eye Hospital, Mary Digby, the Play Specialist, provides the children with *small* scrap-books which they can finish at one sitting. Some children enjoy trimming their own scraps from the Christmas cards, but for others she provides a box of pre-cut ones, small enough to fit the pages of the tiny books. Older children who are not interested in making a scrap-book for themselves like to keep the scrap box topped up.

For a change, try making a place mat. For this, the child needs a rectangle of cardboard. The front of a large packet of Cornflakes or washing powder does beautifully. Cover this with paper, e.g. cheap, coloured sugar paper, or a page from a wallpaper book, and decorate the centre with a doily made from a piece of thin paper. Fold this in half, then in half again. Cut away small pieces here and there from all the folded edges. Open out the paper to reveal the lacy pattern. Stick this to the centre of the place mat and surround it with pictures cut from Christmas cards. With luck, this personal place mat might persuade a messy eater to keep his baked beans on the plate and not scatter them over the table top!

In the Occupational Therapy Department of the Manor Hospital, one of the patients' favourite cutting activities is creating silly pictures! For instance, someone might select a picture of a kitchen, then cut out a horse and stick it in the middle. A man might wear a wheelbarrow on his head, or a house might stand in the middle of a lake. The possibilities are endless, and all good for a laugh!

Egbert, the Egg Box King

Quick

The Manor Hospital, Occupational Therapy Department

If you are looking for a new activity for those with strong hands who are able to cut cardboard, try making a 3D picture of a face using parts of an egg box. Begin with a circle, about the size of a tea plate, drawn on a piece of thin card. This makes the outline of the face, and the features cut from the egg box are glued within it. Two of the recesses in the carton, where the eggs normally sit, make the prominent eyes. One of the spacing pieces, which stops the lid squashing the eggs, makes a long pointed nose, and the mouth and ears are cut from the lid. The King wears a cardboard crown (also cut from the lid) and a frilly paper beard covers his chin. Of course, any character can be made this way. Perhaps a pirate with a patch over one eye, or a posh lady with woolly hair and fancy ear rings made from silver paper!

See also
Dolls, pp. 50–54
Story Books with a Magic Touch, p. 74
Jigsaws, pp. 101–106
Mobiles, pp. 115–120
Posting, pp. 129–131
Threading, pp. 158–160
The Limpet Shell Game, p. 172
Make Your Own Magic Pad, p. 178

ROCK AND ROLL

A Rocking Toy

Quick

Nina Hanson,
Humberside Toy Libraries

Here is a simple rocking toy which many children could make for themselves, or better still, as a present for a younger or less able child to watch. The basis of the toy is the plastic lid from a screw top jar (say from instant coffee). The rim of this lid must be deep enough to rest on its side without toppling over. A picture is mounted or drawn on thin card and glued to the circular surface of the lid (the top when it was on the jar, but now the front). The picture needs to hide as much of the lid as possible and must also protrude a little each side to make two 'levers'. One of these is pressed down and released to start the rocking movement. A picture of a rocking horse or a sailing boat would be a good choice. The rockers of the horse or the hull of the boat could overlap the rim of the lid. A small blob of plasticine inside the lid is necessary to weight the bottom of the toy and make it rock satisfactorily. There is need for experimentation here!

Materials
- A plastic lid with a deep lip
- A suitable picture
- Thin card
- Glue
- A small piece of plasticine

Rock and Roll Tumble Balls

Long-lasting

Jerry Meyerink,
Toy Library Helper,
Walkerton,
Canada

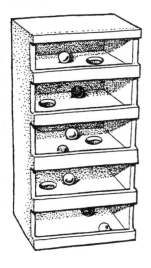

Here is a lovely home-made skill-testing toy that makes you long to have a go! The toy, as it appears in the photograph sent to me by Andrea Lawrence, the toy librarian at Walkerton, Canada, looks like an open-shelved book case. It is about 460 mm high and 250 mm wide. There are four internal shelves, each drilled with a hole which is the right size for a coloured ping-pong ball to drop through. The balls are placed, one at a time, on the top shelf, and the toy is tipped this way and that to guide them through the holes onto the shelves below.

Clearly this is an 'intrigue' toy that can help a child practise hand-eye coordination and have a lot of fun into the bargain. It requires both hands to tip the box, and careful aim is needed to navigate the balls through the holes. The toy, as illustrated, shows two simple adaptations which could bring it within the capabilities of many children who might otherwise find it too difficult to manipulate. The back has been covered over to prevent the balls from falling out that way, and there is a narrow strip of wood in front of each shelf to stop them from falling forward. When a ball has finished its journey to the bottom, the player can easily reach in and start it off again at the top.

This toy can be enlarged for 'tough guys', if tennis balls are substituted for ping-pong balls. It can be scaled down to take marbles. With a piece of perspex across the front to seal them in, it makes a good one-piece toy to help while away a long journey. When all the marbles reach the bottom, simply invert the box and start again!

SHAPES
SMELL
SPEECH
STACKING

SHAPES

Shapes Busy Board

Long-lasting

Erica Watson,
Hospital Play Specialist

All the commercial shapes boards on offer seem to belong to one of two categories. Either the loose pieces must be fitted into the matching recess, or they must be placed over the correct peg. This home-made shapes board combines both these ideas. The word 'busy' in the title is meant to suggest that this toy is more than just a shape-matching exercise. In the hands of an ingenious child, each shape can also be a plaything.

The board was designed for use in a hospital ward. In this situation, as in a toy library, a toy which (a) intrigues, (b) is easy to use (in bed, on the floor, or at a table), (c) is interesting for a fairly wide age range and (d) can be easily checked and cleaned, must surely be a useful addition to the toy cupboard.

The picture shows the way the shapes are arranged. At the top of the board are two pegs. The short one holds the circle and the longer one is needed for the three graded squares which form a pyramid. Colour matching is introduced here. Around the base of each peg is painted the shape it should receive. Red for the circle, green for the three squares. The circle can be spun on its peg like a top and the squares can be stacked in different ways, perhaps the smallest first.

The triangle (coloured yellow) and the oblong (blue) are cut out of the base board. This must then be backed with hardboard to stop the shapes dropping through. The triangle lifts out with a tiny picture ring. This is intended to encourage fine finger movements. Of course, an alternative could be used. The bottom of the recess is lined with sandpaper and this distinctive tex-

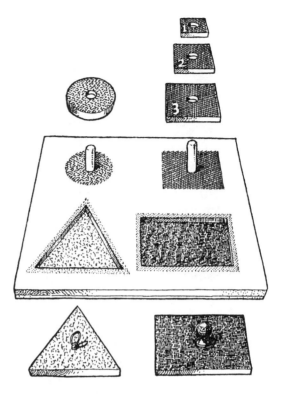

ture is also glued to the underside of the triangle shape. If you fear a busy child might use this to rub the polish off the table just use another texture! The bottom of the oblong recess is lined with blue felt to make a soft bed for the mirror card which is stuck to the underside of the shape. This has a cupboard doorknob on the top which makes it easy to manipulate. It can be used just as a mirror, or perhaps, on a bright day, it can reflect the sunshine and throw a 'Jack-a-dandy' on the ceiling.

Materials

- A piece of plywood for the base board (300 x 380 mm).
- A smaller piece of plywood. From this cut the circle (100 mm diameter) and three squares (100, 80 and 60 mm). All these shapes need a hole drilled in the centre.
- A piece of hardboard also 300 x 380 mm to back the base board.
- A small piece of dowel. (The diameter of this determines the size of the holes above.)

- A cupboard doorknob for the oblong.
- A picture ring, or alternative, for the triangle.
- Two triangles of sandpaper, the same size as the shape (each side 110 mm).
- Blue felt for the oblong recess (50 x 150 mm).
- Mirror card for the underside of the oblong.
- Humbrol Enamel: red, green, yellow and blue.
- Polyurethane varnish to protect all the pieces and make them easy to clean.

The suggested dimensions can, of course, be altered. Before making the proper toy, it is a wise plan to cut the board and all the shapes out of rough paper. It is easy then to make any alterations you want.

A Silhouette Shapes Bingo

Quick

R.L.

This is a shapes-matching game that can be useful for a group of mixed ability. The crèche at the toy library has been busy all morning, but with only half an hour to go before closing time four children remain. They are an interesting little bunch. Jason, a mathematical wizard for his age, uses words like 'conical' and 'rectangular' appropriately in his conversation and is probably heading for a career in nuclear physics! Mary is shy and quiet. She usually prefers to play alongside other children rather than with them. Peter, the youngest, has Down's Syndrome and is doing well. His latest achievement has been to put the circle, square and triangle into a form board entirely on his own. Emma can now manage any game suitable for a four-year-old thanks to her new contact lenses. The crèche helpers have their eye on the clock and are thinking of all the toy checking, cleaning and putting away that lies before them. One agrees to take the children into a quiet corner to try out a recently made game of Shapes Bingo, so that the others can start the chores.

The children are interested in the new box, and Peter, as the youngest, is given the honour of removing the lid. Inside is the usual collection of base boards marked into squares which have to be filled appropriately. Instead of picture cards or numbers, this game has a bag full of coloured shapes which have to be matched to a corresponding silhouette on the base boards. This is quite a new idea for the children who, up to now, have always matched identical pictures. They must look carefully to make sure each black shape is properly covered. They have a quick trial run and soon discover an oval is not the same as a circle and a square will not cover an oblong.

On this particular morning, there are eight boards for only four children. Rather than spend time in sorting out four sets, the helper shares them all among the children. Peter is given one with the shapes he knows so well. Emma has two boards on the table in front of her, at a comfortable distance for her to see easily. Mary, Jason and the helper look after the rest. Each player dips into the shapes bag in turn. The piece taken out is discussed and given to whoever needs it for their board. (Note this deviation from the normal rules where *one* person calls out all the pieces and does not fill a board. Anyone can win, but the game is only over when the bag is empty and *all* the boards are full.)

Because this game is unusual in that coloured shapes (some simple, others complicated) have to be matched to a silhouette, it has an appeal for intelligent children like Jason. For slow learners or children who don't see too clearly, covering a black shape with a coloured one makes it obvious which pieces still have to be collected, and the filled board looks satisfyingly colourful and complete.

See also
A Tactile Posting Box, p. 130

SMELL

A Pot Pourri of Delectable Smells

Instant

Angela Smith,
Teacher,
Special Care Unit,
Walton Leigh School

Angela has a large bag designated to receive any pleasantly aromatic object she comes across in her daily life. She has a constantly changing supply of 'goodies' she can call upon whenever she decides to hold a sniffing session. She sits the children in a circle. In the background the tape recorder plays soft music while each object is passed slowly round the circle for each child in turn to sniff appreciatively for as long as she pleases. Meanwhile, the other children can enjoy the

An Aromatic Herbaceous Border

Quick

Margaret Gilman and the
    Nursery Staff,
White Lodge Spastics Centre

music and watch each other's reactions. A good idea this, for it makes sure the children have a pause between each smell – to follow one with another in quick succession can dull the effect.

Angela's bag is a treasure trove of bottles, jars and tins from which she can select the perfumes of the day. Close fitting lids help the smells to stay fresh and not intermingle. She uses hand cream which can be rubbed gently onto the backs of the children's hands (good also for body awareness!). She has real food, herbs etc., in screw top jars, crunchy plastic potato crisp bags (smoky bacon is the favourite), and of course plenty of bottles of perfume, tins of talc etc.

The staff make tissue paper flowers with cotton wool centres sprinkled with scent to add colour and perfume to the classroom. When they are not being used for decorative purposes, they can be given to the children to hold, or wear as an outsize buttonhole. A child celebrating a birthday may have a garland of them draped round her wheelchair.

Each flower is made from a pipe cleaner, a small ball of cotton wool and some tissue paper in eye-catching colours. Margaret gave me one as a sample, which I promptly vandalised to see how it was made! The dimensions given make a flower *about* 140 mm across. Make one to get the knack, then adjust the size as you wish.

Fold the pipe cleaner in half, push the cotton wool tightly against the half-way bend and twist the pipe cleaner to hold it firmly in the middle. Cut two different coloured pieces of tissue paper about 140 mm square. Lay one on top of the other, and pleat them together, creasing them one way, then the other, zig-zag fashion, as though you were making a fan. Keeping the pleats together, fold the paper in half. With your scissors round off the sharp corners at the open ends. Open out the strip of pleats (still keeping it as a strip) and push it between the ends of the pipe cleaner, hard against the cotton wool. Twist up the pipe cleaner as tightly as possible to squeeze the tissue paper and keep it in place. Tease out the pleats until each half of the flower is like a semicircular fan. Join them together with a dab of glue. Bend up the sharp ends of the pipe cleaners, and bind the stalk with masking tape. Lastly, sprinkle a little perfume on the cotton wool.

Materials
- A packet of pipe cleaners
- Some cotton wool balls
- Tissue paper in various bright colours
- Masking tape
- Perfume

A Tough Smelly Toy

Long-lasting

Graham Merrett and Richard Stewart,
Teachers

When Graham was a student at a school for autistic children, he noticed the way the sense of smell seemed to be particularly important to the pupils. Some would smell an object even before they looked at it. He felt that such instinctive behaviour could be turned to good effect if the children could be given a toy where the sense of smell was all important. Such toys do not exist in the shops, so necessity became the mother of invention.

There is a well-known sound-matching activity where a quantity of identical containers are arranged in twos. A different filling is put in each pair (bells, rice, pebbles, coins, etc.) All the containers are then muddled up and the child gives each a good shake to distinguish between the sounds to enable him to pair them all up again. Graham in conjunction with his tutor, Richard Stewart, devised a smell-pairing activity on the lines of this idea. For the containers, he used plumbers' plastic piping, stops ends and connectors (available from builders' merchants). He cut the piping into short lengths and drilled holes in it to let out the smell. A stop end was glued to one end of each piece, using the correct adhesive, also obtained from the builders' merchants. The other end was blocked off with a cork (from a shop selling home brewing equipment). The corked end of *one* of each pair of containers was fitted with a connector. A line was drawn with marker pen along the connector and the tube it should receive. As an added guide, a small notch (different in shape for each pair) was cut from the connector, and the piece taken out applied to the matching tube. When they were joined together, using the guide line to line them up, they fitted

145

perfectly, proving to the child that he had paired the smells correctly.

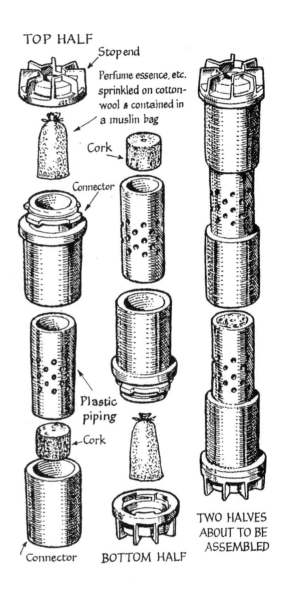

TOP HALF
Stop end
Perfume essence, etc. sprinkled on cotton-wool & contained in a muslin bag
Cork
Connector
Plastic piping
Cork
Connector
BOTTOM HALF
TWO HALVES ABOUT TO BE ASSEMBLED

The smells were contained in removable muslin bags, closed by Velcro flaps, and then inserted into the tubes through the stop ends which could be unscrewed for the purpose. The bags were easy to clean and refill. Liquids such as peppermint essence were dropped onto cotton wool. Other smells used were coffee grounds, soap powder, bath crystals, mixed herbs and after-shave lotion!

I tried out this idea with a group of slow learners. My aim was to encourage them to concentrate on using their sense of smell, and hopefully, to enjoy the experience. My version of the 'toy' was a modestly small one, using only three sets of smells, which I felt to be sufficient for the purpose I had in mind. At first, I used far too much smell in each tube. The whole room was filled with a cocktail of soap powder, peppermint and coffee! I also discovered, the hard way, that at the end of each session every pair of containers must be stored separately, or all the smells will intermingle. If this happens, it is no great disaster, for the 'toy' is extremely easy to wash, and can soon be refilled. My version lacked Graham's self-correcting feature of the notch and piece to fit in. I was not sure my technical skills could cope with such accurate cutting, and for my purpose it seemed unnecessary. The activity worked very well once I had learnt to provide a mere whiff of each smell. It can be quite painful to take a hearty sniff of strong peppermint! We found that part of the fun was finding out if the smells had been matched correctly, and I am sure the adults enjoyed running their noses along the tubes just as much as the children did.

This 'toy' is very tough, and will last virtually for ever, but keep it out of the hands of children who throw!

SPEECH

Lollipops to Talk to

Quick

Lekotek Korea,
The Toy Library,
Seoul

Here is a delightful idea from half way round the world. It makes imaginative use of photographs of members of the family. These seem to have a magnetic attraction for all children, so anyone who takes the small amount of trouble needed to make this activity should hope for plenty of spontaneous vocalising and speech. Once the idea has proved its worth, the stock of lollipops can be extended to include pets, the family car, friends, and even picture postcards of places visited.

The photographs are stuck on the front of pieces of cardboard, about the size of an adult's hand. Each piece is cut a different shape. The square piece could be for Dad's photograph, the circle for Mum, the diamond for the child in question, the triangle for the baby, and so on. A handle is fixed to the back of each shape. In Korea, they use a chopstick, but a strip of thick card or a lolly stick would do just as well. Fix it on firmly with Sellotape or glue. The handle is a necessity. It can protrude over the edge of the table and make it easier for the child to lift the shape. It also makes sure the picture will be looked at the right way up!

There are plenty of ways of playing with these 'lolli-pops'. At first, they will probably be lifted in turn, the photograph examined and the person named. Then the child can be asked to find Daddy, say 'Hello Daddy' and so on through the family. Another time 'Good-bye Daddy' (etc.) can be added as each 'lollipop' is returned to the table, face downwards. An imaginative adult will find ways of using the child's existing vocabulary and extending it as the 'lollipop' sessions continue. In Korea, the more vocal children are encouraged to hold a conversation between two of the photographs. This must surely spur on the imagination of a child who already has plenty of words at his disposal!

Materials
- Photographs of members of the family
- Cardboard shapes; a different one for each photo-graph

- A handle to stick on the back of each
- An optional extra — felt pens or coloured paper to decorate the backs of the shapes

Mr Murphy's Boxes

Quick

Mr Murphy,
Home Teacher of young deaf children

Picture a collection of shoeboxes, each labelled with the name of a day of the week. Lift any lid, and inside you will find pictures and tiny toys relating to a particular topic such as 'transport' or 'the seaside'. There is a different subject for every day of the week. As the contents of the boxes are easily added to or changed, here is a possible answer to the problem of how to hold a child's interest, encourage him to use the words he already knows, and to learn new ones. Mr Murphy's boxes make daily speech sessions an occasion to welcome favourite old toys or to be surprised by new ones. Week after week, each box can be used on its appropriate day. As the contents are lifted out, one by one, they are named and talked about. For instance, Monday might be farm day. Inside the appropriate box could be a farm picture-book and some lifelike plastic animals. As each one is taken from the box (a lucky dip?), it is named, described, its cry imitated etc. Helping the animals to stand up encourages taking care, and nimble fingers. The picture-book can be looked at, and again the animals named. Next Monday the farm stock could be arranged in groups with the dog rounding up the sheep and the ducks waddling in line, or the plastic animals could be matched to those in the picture-book. Another Monday, a sheet of paper, some crayons and a tea box might be added to the collection. Now a simple farm layout can be made, so that the ducks swim on the pond, the cows graze in the meadow and the horse surveys the scene from his tea box stable.

The shoebox for Tuesdays might hold small objects relating to the house (doll's house furniture comes in handy here) — all to be *talked about* and played with. Perhaps the idea of making a scrap-book about houses and furniture could follow. This will mean searching together for suitable pictures in mail order catalogues and magazines. On Wednesdays, words relating to garments might be the choice. Explore inside the box for ordinary or dressing-up clothes; or you might find a doll to dress appropriately with vest and pants first!

And so on through the week. I leave you to fill the remaining boxes!

Materials

Really, this activity requires no making at all, merely the labelling of the shoeboxes and the collection of the items to put in them for each particular day. This last part requires thought, and possibly quite a lot of time to assemble enough interesting things for a session or each day of the week. If the prospect seems daunting start small, just filling a box for, say, Tuesdays and Thursdays. You are sure to find these boxes add to the enjoyment and value of speech sessions on these days – so hurry up and fill some more!

Note. If you are playing with a profoundly handicapped child, who has no speech, these boxes can still be useful. If you put a different collection of toys in each you will have a variety of stimulation material ready to hand which will avoid the boredom (for you) of using the same things every day. Each box might contain a toy to encourage eye tracking, a special rattle, a feely toy something nice to smell, a 'tickling' stick, a home-made scrap-book etc.

Where Does it Go?

Quick

Catherine O'Neil,
Speech Therapist

This useful device has been designed to help young children with a language delay, but it could also be of benefit to many slow learners. Its purpose is to encourage the child to sort out a collection of objects related to themes and put them into their right categories. Catherine's choice was food, furniture and zoo animals.

She made a hinged, fold-away screen from three large panels of cardboard. In the centre of each was a hole about the size of a saucer, with a plastic bag behind it fixed with staples or sticky tape. This made a pocket to hold all the bits and pieces the child would post into it. A picture was drawn round each hole to show what category of object the bag behind it should receive: a house, with the hole forming a large upstairs circular window for the furniture; a gate in the wall of the zoo for the animals; and a shopping basket for the food. A cardboard panel was hinged each side of the central one using strong plastic tape or carpet binding. When the sides were bent back the three pieces formed a stable triangle which stood on the floor. Now all that was needed was a box full of doll's house furniture, zoo animals and *pictures* of food. (Using the real thing would cause problems!) The child was given (or chose) an item from the box. His attention was focused on this while he looked at it, named it, talked about it and finally posted it in the right hole.

Materials
- Three panels of cardboard, say 600 mm x 900 mm
- Plastic tape or carpet binding for the hinges
- Three strong plastic bags
- Staples or plastic tape (for fixing the bags in place)
- Felt pens for drawing the clue-pictures round the holes
- A box full of objects to be categorised

In a more robust form with plywood or hardboard sides, this toy could be well worth including in the stock of a toy library. It folds away flat and provides another way of helping any child with a language problem to learn new words and practise those he knows already.

For more ideas from Catherine *see* the Special Needs Catalogue, p. 189.

A Successful DIY First Lotto

Quick

R.L.

Games such as picture dominoes or lotto, where the essence of the game is looking carefully at a picture and then matching it to an identical one, can always be made to produce many opportunities for talking – at the simplest level, just naming the objects on the cards, and progressing from there to describing, comparing, and so on. Although there are many excellent sets of lotto and dominoe games commercially available, they are not suitable for all children. They may have too many pieces, or the vocabulary needed might be too complicated. When I was working with a group of slow learners I devised a 'training' lotto game. This was intended to help the children practise a limited list of words, and to understand the idea of matching an individual picture card to a corresponding one on the base board. It is not possible to buy a lotto like this, but it is simplicity itself to make. Its special feature is that the small picture is placed *beside* the one on the base board, not on top of it as happens with every bought game. The great advantage of this arrangement is that it is obvious to everybody when a picture has been matched correctly. Should one player make a mistake, all the others are certain to tell him about it, and help him to put it right!

To make a game for four players, you will need six sheets of stout cardboard (I used the fronts and backs of three large washing powder packets), and some pairs of matching pictures. If, like me, you are not a confident artist, it is possible to buy small coloured pictures from educational suppliers (e.g. Philip and Tacey, p. 189) or you can use the pictures from a sheet of suitable gift wrapping paper. Put two sheets of cardboard to one side. They will be needed to mount the matching pictures. Rule out pairs of squares on each of the four remaining pieces of cardboard to form the base boards. Stick a picture on the left hand square of each pair. The blank squares on the right are for the matching pictures which are mounted on the two spare sheets of cardboard, and cut out ready for play.

The rules of the game can easily be adapted to fit the ability of the group playing. In our case, all the cards were placed face downwards in the centre of the table. The players examined the pictures on their base boards, and together we named each one, sometimes making comments like 'yum yum' for the icecream, or 'Mary has blue shoes'. Then each child, in turn, would take a card from the top of the pile, look at it and say its name. The card was given to the player who required it and everyone checked to see if he had claimed correctly and watched him place it beside the matching picture on his base board – and so on round the table until every board was filled to our satisfaction. When the children could confidently play the game in this basic way, it was time to introduce a variation. Perhaps a card would be picked up, not shown to the children, but the question asked 'Who would like the hat?' The child with that picture on his base board needed to remember the name without the help of the picture before he replied, 'Me please'. The same game was used with a more advanced group. This time a clue was given, e.g. 'Who would like something green and yellow that you could wear on your head?'

Note. From the post-Christmas glut of used cards, it is often possible to find two the same. Collect enough pairs and you have a free set of matching pictures!

I Packed My Suitcase

An Instant Group Game, but items need to be collected in advance

The very best time to play this game is before a journey when a group of children are thinking about what to take, and packing the suitcase is all part of the excitement. At other times, it can be a useful way of practising the vocabulary associated with clothes and of consolidating the use of these words in a different context. It is a cumulative game, each player adding another word to the list, so it is wise to arrange for the more able players to have the later turns!

First find a large container. The Feely Box on p. 72 is ideal, but you could also use a sports bag or a pillow case – in fact, anything that will keep all the contents hidden. Then collect a variety of clothes (and perhaps toilet requirements or toys) that might be taken on holiday. In turn, each child has a 'lucky dip' in the container. The first one says: 'I packed my suitcase and I put in (dips in) a shoe.' The second repeats the sentence and adds the garment he pulls out, 'I packed my suitcase and I put in a shoe . . . and a jersey!' The third child says all this and adds his contribution. So the list of clothing gets longer with each turn until the container is empty.

I have seen this game played at a simpler level with a group of children in a special class. The ritual sentence was beyond them, but some could name items of clothing. Making sure everything was marked (!), the teacher put everyone's going-home clothes in a big box. As each article was taken out, it was named by everyone and given to the correct child to put on. Dressing the children this way might take a little longer, but it turned a daily chore into an interesting learning activity.

The suitcase game has many variations, such as 'I went shopping and I bought . . .' (dip in a shopping bag to find out what) or 'I went to the Zoo and I saw . . .' (plastic animals can be used for this version). In a more difficult form, it is called the memory game. You may have played it at a party. The players sit in a circle. The first one says a noun, e.g. 'coat'. The second player repeats this and adds a word of his own, e.g. 'coat, button'. Next turn might be: 'coat, button, mushroom'. Each player contributes his own word to the list, which gets longer until finally the chain of words breaks when someone finds it is impossible to remember them all!

Getting it Wrong Again!

Instant

Lorraine Crawford,
Speech Therapist,
The Manor Hospital

If you want to add a touch of hilarity to the day, try the game Lorraine sometimes uses. She has a box full of dressing-up clothes handy, and in front of a group of patients *she* chooses a garment and deliberately puts it on wrongly — back to front, upside down, inside out, shoes on her hands, socks on her ears! There is no end to the possibilities, and you can imagine the laughter and speech this game sparks off.

STACKING

Higher and Higher

Quick

Lekotek Korea,
The Toy Library, Seoul

Children with poor hand control seldom *choose* to play with a stacking toy. It is difficult and frustrating for them to try to pile one object on top of another, and to place a part of a toy accurately over a stacking rod is often quite impossible (e.g. the fish in the 'tropical aquarium', p. 156).

154

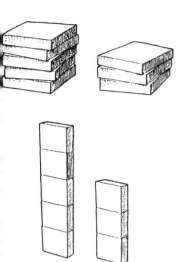

Here is an easily made stacking toy which does away with all this failure. It is nothing more than a collection of flat wooden bricks, but it really works. The child may not be able to place the bricks precisely enough to make a nice tidy pile, but he will have a good chance of making a really high tower and so end up with a pleasant glow of achievement. In the process, he will have practised hand-eye coordination, and the skill of grasping and releasing.

These useful bricks can be made from any spare pieces of plywood, blockboard or high density fibre board with the edges sanded to remove roughness and possible splinters. They must be thick enough to be picked up easily, and a suitable size to fit the user's hands, say 90 mm.

If the bricks are cut accurately, a nimble-fingered child can try stacking them end on. This takes considerable skill.

A special set of stacking bricks was tried out with a young man attending a Day Centre. He was a big lad, well over six foot tall, with correspondingly large hands. His movements were quick and careless. He did not give himself time to think about what he was doing, so usually had to do it twice! If he was asked to hang up his anorak, he would toss it at the wall, near the peg and, of course, it just fell down again. Every activity he undertook seemed to be finished in two seconds flat, because he never stopped to *look carefully* at what he was doing. We tried slowing him down a little by giving him a good supply of these bricks. In his case, they were cut particularly small, about 30 mm square. By the end of the week, he could balance nearly all the bricks on top of each other, and really enjoyed the challenge. This young man also happened to be colour blind, so his stacking squares were painted black on one side and white on the other. This made them more versatile and able to be used also for sorting, matching and making simple patterns, like the alternate black and white squares on a draught board.

155

A Tropical Aquarium

Long-lasting

Mr Poedjangga,
Indonesia

A student from Indonesia who attended a course at HEARU (Handicap, Education and Aids Research Unit, City of London Polytechnic) has made this clever stacking toy.

Three chunky fish locate over short lengths of dowel fixed to a base board. (If necessary this can be clamped to the table for even more stability.) The first fish is left intact. The others are divided by a wiggly saw cut into two and three pieces, respectively, making them into

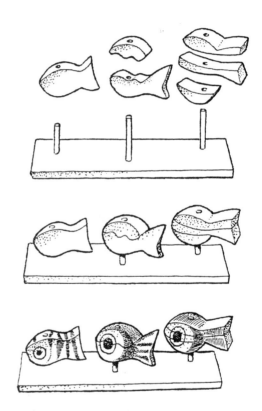

mini-jigsaws. Each fish is attractively painted in bright colours. Because of the thickness of the wood, the pieces are easy to handle. Putting these fish together correctly may be possible for children who find it hard to 'grasp and release'. This attractive toy can be used to encourage children to practise all the skills of stacking, counting and colour matching. Every toy library should have one!

Materials
- A base board, say 350 x 150 x 20 mm
- Three short lengths of doweling
- A piece of 38 mm thick soft wood for the fish
- Paint, (i.e. Humbrol Enamel)
- Polyurethane varnish to protect

Stack anything

The following ideas have come from Pam Courtney, Christine Cousins and Kanji Watenabi, who works with disabled children in Japan:

- Stones with flat surfaces, washed smooth by the sea. As an optional extra, these can be coloured.
- Saucepans.
- Flower pots.
- Matchboxes.
- Cotton reels.
- Egg cups.
- Limpet shells (difficult!).
- Yogurt pots or plastic cups.
- Christmas cards: the first one opened out as though it was being displayed on the mantelpiece, the second one lying horizontally across it, the third one standing on that, etc.

See also
Build a Town, p. 30
Giant Tactile Dominoes, p. 71

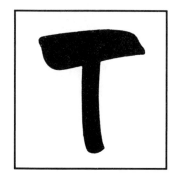

THREADING

THROWING

THREADING

Threading is a peaceful activity with many useful spin-offs. It encourages the use of both hands as well as hand-eye coordination. Colour matching, counting, and even sorting and grading can be introduced. Apart from all these worthy attributes, most children find threading enjoyable.

First of all the skill of just poking the threader through the hole must be learnt.

- In an Australian toy library, the children begin by threading large hair curlers onto a piece of hose-pipe.
- At Lekotek Korea, they have large wooden blocks with holes through them, and a piece of dowel to use as a threader. Blocks with smaller holes are provided as the child's skill increases.
- At some toy libraries in the UK the children follow Roy McConkey's suggestion and thread plastic rings, cut from a washing-up liquid bottle, over a broom handle.

The next stage is to string a number of things together to make a necklace. My favourite first 'bead' is made from the cardboard (or plastic) tube from the inside of a till roll – in common use at the checkout at the local supermarket. Ask nicely, and the checkout staff will be delighted to give them to you! These tubes have a *large* central hole. They are about 60 mm long and are very strong. All this makes them a great improvement on the cotton reels we have been using for years. Suitably painted and given a protective coat of Polyurethane varnish, the till rolls can look very attractive. If they are made 'two tone' with one half painted, say, red and the other half yellow, the children can use their colour matching skills to thread them dominoe fashion, matching colour to colour. This idea was first used at a toy library at Oxford.

The best threader at this stage is a length of plastic washing line – the sort without a wire core.

Beads made from short lengths of bamboo are a useful intermediate stage between till rolls and commercial beads. They are lovely for older children who may not be able to manage the fine threading necessary to make themselves a necklace from plastic or wooden beads. They are also light in weight and could appeal to children who need 'low effort' toys. So if you are looking for something for a child to thread which is strong, light and with a large hole, read on.

The beads are made from ordinary bamboo cane used for staking plants in the garden. First, scrape off the waxy coating from the outside of the bamboo, so that you can paint it later on. Then cut the bamboo into small pieces about 20–30 mm long, or as you wish, (avoiding the joints) and poke out the pith that is inside. Give all the pieces a rub with sandpaper to make sure they are smooth and pleasant to feel. They are now ready for painting. If you want to indulge your artistic talent and have the time and patience, the beads can be decorated elaborately with little flowers, animals or patterns, and the end result will be really attractive. Don't forget to apply a coat of protective Polyurethane varnish.

Now the skill of threading has been learnt, a child can really go to town! At first just making a long string of beads will be pleasing, but I think any industrious threader must feel a little disheartened when she sees her morning's work taken apart and tipped back into the box at the end of the session. How much more fun to make something to keep or to give to someone as a little present. Here are some ideas. She might:

- thread milkbottle tops and macaroni alternately, to make a rustly curtain, or to dangle from a mobile;

- thread squares of stale toast, or peanuts in their husks, or strings of raisins, and hang them up for the birds;
- make a necklace for a doll, or a bracelet for herself by threading short lengths of plastic drinking straws onto a pipe cleaner.

Threading can also be a preparation for simple sewing. You can make a first sewing card by drawing the outline of a picture (e.g., house, cat, flower) on a polystyrene food packaging tray and punching holes at intervals around the edge of the picture. An easy way to do this is to support the tray on a soft surface such as a carpet with a deep pile, and prod it with a knitting needle. Now all is ready for the child to poke a bodkin, threaded with brightly coloured wool, in and out of the holes to outline the picture. The rim of the tray makes a ready-made frame, so the completed picture can be hung on the wall for all to admire.

On similar lines, a personal treasure bag can be made from an old Christmas card. The child selects the card. Holes are punched at the sides and bottom, but not at the top, for this is left open to receive the 'treasures'. Using a bodkin and thick wool, the child can thread in and out of the holes to turn the card into a pocket. The ends of the wool are joined together to form a handle over the top.

See also
Straw Dancing Dolly, p. 52
Rustly Mobile, p. 117

THROWING

Polystyrene Plane

Quick

Thinking back to our childhood, we can all remember the delight of throwing and chasing paper darts, and the physical and mental effort we put into trying to make them go farther with every flight. John has contributed a design for a more robust version which, with luck, will both go farther and last longer.

John Gould,
Lecturer,
Play Equipment Design,
London College of Furniture

USE STANDARD FLAME-RETARDANT
12 INCH FOAM CEILING TILE.
USE SHARP CRAFT KNIFE WITH
BLADE HELD AT LOW ANGLE
WHEN CUTTING

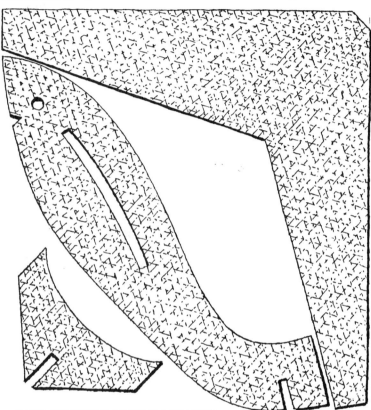

NOSE WEIGHTED WITH PLASTICINE
SQUEEZED INTO HOLE OR NOTCH.
EXPERIMENT BY ADDING AND SUBTRACTING
VERY SMALL QUANTITIES.

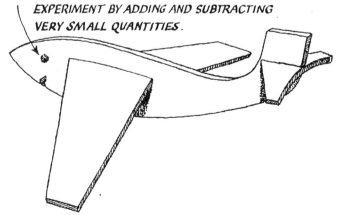

The plane is designed to be cut from a 12 in poly-styrene ceiling tile. The leading edges of the wings lie along two sides of the tile and the fuselage and tail are cut from the remainder. Small blobs of plasticine can be added to the nose in the places indicated to adjust the balance for perfect flight.

Because of the lightness of the materials used, this plane can be played with indoors, but for maximum activity use it outside on a calm day.

Beanbags With a Difference

Quick

R.L.

Games of throw and catch are always popular, but for some children, playing with a ball may not be possible. Using a beanbag may be the answer. This is usually about 75 x 130 mm and is filled with dried peas or rice. If you make your own from any strong, colourful material, both the size and the weight of the beanbag can be at your discretion. For a heavier filling (which some children find easier to control), I have used 'fish grit', i.e. the gravel that can be bought cheaply in pet shops and is used to line the bottoms of fish tanks. This has the added advantage of being washable (unlike rice or peas!) so, if the 'bean' bag is accidentally left out in the rain or dropped in the paddling pool, no harm is done.

At the other extreme, if you want a large and light beanbag, make a jumbo case and fill it with polystyrene chips. This idea was passed on to me by Monica Taylor at the Rix Toy Library, Normansfield. She makes cylindrical cushions about 300 mm long with removable (and washable) outer covers. These are used for games of throw and catch with groups of slow learners, some in wheelchairs. A large, extra light rustly beanbag like this is also excellent to use with visually handicapped children. It is quite harmless should they fail to catch it, but if they are successful, they have the added reward of the pleasant feel and sound.

Another Target Game

Instant

Roy McConkey

In one of his lectures Roy McConkey, an expert on play for children with special needs, suggested an instant throwing game packed full of activity. It can be played by two people at any time, anywhere, for all it requires is a carrier bag and a modest supply of scrap-paper. The paper is folded into paper darts, and one player hurls these into a carrier bag held open by the other. The bag man aims to catch as many darts as possible. Remembering the erratic flight of most paper darts, the catcher must *watch* the approaching missile and move nimbly to trap it in his bag.

Two sock games for letting off steam

Sock Fights

Instant
For two or more

Maureen McEvoy

This game bears a strong resemblance to the ever popular one of pillow-fighting. The advantage of this version is that the 'biffer' is considerably smaller and, therefore, less likely to damage either player or property! To make a 'biffer' all you need do is to put a foam ball (or a handful of cotton wool balls) in the toe of an old sock and tie a knot half way up the leg. This will keep the stuffing in place.

Any rules must be understood before battle commences. It is as well to encourage biffing only below shoulder height. The head area *must* be out of bounds if glasses are worn, and hits there must be heavily penalised, perhaps with a trip to the 'sin bin'?

Human Skittles

Instant
Group game

R.L.

This game was invented at a home for mentally handicapped children. It involved a great deal of controlled activity and movement, and soon became the top favourite 'busy' game. It was played in the games room where the odd wild throw could do no damage. All it required was a large quantity of odd socks (donated by the care staff and topped up from time to time) and a box to keep them in. Each sock was rolled up into a ball. (A good activity for encouraging manual dexterity!) It did not matter if they came unrolled in flight – they were just less likely to reach the target and could soon be rerolled for the next go.

The players were divided into two groups, the 'skittles' and the 'throwers'. (Sometimes children v staff, sometimes mixed groups.) The 'skittles' stood stiffly at one end of the room with their backs to the 'throwers', who had to keep their distance by making sure their toes were behind the edge of the carpet. When a 'skittle' was hit, it had to topple to the ground, and when all were down, the teams changed places. It usually took some time and

considerable searching to reclaim all the socks. Plenty of bending and stretching needed for this activity!

The game was noisy and lively, but also disciplined. The box of socks could not be raided until both teams were in place, and throwing had to wait until the umpire said the ritual, 'One, two, three, GO!'

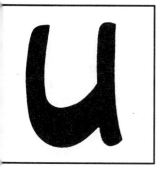

USEFUL HINTS

Stabilising toys

The Special Needs Information Pack, available from *Play Matters*, the National Toy Libraries Association, is crammed full of useful tips and suggests solutions to many problems. It is a *must* for anyone running a toy library for children with special needs. For anyone concerned with helping individual children, here are three suggestions from it. They all deal with ways of anchoring toys, and are available from Boots. They can be ordered at the pharmacy and should be delivered within 14 days.

- *Stay-put Pad*. This is about 100 mm in diameter. Press it onto a flat surface. Put the toy on top and rotate it. This will form a vacuum with the pad. To remove the toy, turn it in the opposite direction.
- *Plate Holder*. This is a double-faced suction pad.
- *Non-slip Pad*. This measures 250 x 85 mm. It sticks to a flat surface and will hold any object placed on it.

More tips

- Boat chandlers sell attractive trays with a non-slip surface for use on yachts. They make splendid non-slip toy trays!
- Dychem is a non-slip plastic material available in various circle sizes and in a sheet. It is available from various sources including Boots and Nottingham Rehab Ltd (*see* list of Manufacturers, p. 189).

- Magnetic tape and magnets in general are useful for holding objects to a metal surface. Available from Hestair Hope and others, *see* pp. 187–190. The tape has an adhesive surface and can be applied to wood or cardboard. If you have some wooden templates, of animals for instance, which look unattractive because they are covered with scribble, try painting them on one side. Protect the surface with a coat of Polyurethane and apply a few small strips of magnetic tape to the underside. They can then be used on a metal surface (perhaps a storage cupboard?) to make a farm scene.
- Some toys can be mounted on a larger wooden base and clamped to the table.
- Small therapy sandbags are useful for weighting or wedging toys to keep them stable.

Don't forget the low technology!

It's amazing what you can do with Velcro, string, tape, bulldog clips, clothes pegs, Sellotape, Blu-tack, Sticky Fixers, masking tape, a brick wrapped in cloth or a pile of old telephone directories.

- Playing cards can be poked into the bristles of a scrubbing brush.
- Flat-bottomed toys can be made to stay in place by pushing them firmly onto a damp suction-pad soap holder.
- A simple storage bag can be made from a circle of material with curtain rings and a drawstring round the edge. The bag, perhaps containing building bricks, can be spread out flat and used as a play cloth. When playtime ends, the drawstring can be tightened, and all the bricks are again contained in the bag.
- To concentrate a child's attention on the play in progress, it can sometimes help to use a *cold* tin camping plate as a play surface.
- Use Loet Vos' Instant Dolls (p. 50) strung on elastic, to make a cot or pram toy.

- If you need very tough toys for children who chew, try the pet shop and see what is on offer for the puppies!

- Oven gloves make good instant glove puppets for older children with adult-sized hands.

- For children who cannot manage to use a paint brush, try filling an empty roll-on deodorant stick with paint of a suitable consistency – thickish, but flowing.

- A door stop on a spring makes a delightful 'doodle' toy. It can be screwed to a busy board, table top etc.

- Add foil diffraction paper (available from Edu-play, *see* p. 187) to toys with moving parts, such as Coggipegs. This adds to their attraction for children with a visual handicap.

- Where children are unable to see pictures mounted on the wall, take a tip from the teachers at the White Lodge Spastics Centre and try mounting them on the ceiling, or even on the floor.

Ideas contributed by Margaret Gilman, Freda Kim, Susan Myatt, Advisors to the RNIB, The Sense Centre, Ealing, students attending the Toy Making Course at the London College of Furniture, Alison Wisbeach.

See also
Part I: Creating the Conditions for Play, pp. 1–22

VISUAL STIMULATION

Two ideas for children who do not like to make eye contact

Pam Courtney (teacher) says: make your own face spectacular! You can do this by using face paints, perhaps giving yourself a large red spot on the end of your nose and thick black eyebrows. Alternatively, you might wear an illuminated head band bought at a fair or joke shop.

Susan Myatt (parent) says: play Hidey Boo down a tunnel. Cover the child's head with a tablecloth. Lift up one edge so that the cloth covers your head too, and say 'Boo'! The only place the child can look is down the tunnel, at your smiling face!

Tips for children with a visual handicap

Pam Courtney (teacher) says: if a visually handicapped child is lying on the floor, encourage all the family to wear fluorescent socks!

Mary Digby (Play Specialist) says: add interesting sparkle to wooden bricks of various shapes and sizes. Cover them with diffraction paper (from Edu-Play, *see* p. 187). It can be stuck on with double-sided Sellotape. At playtime, put the bricks on a dark surface, e.g. a board covered with black felt, and place them in a strong light for the shiny surfaces to have maximum effect.

Shirley Fiddler (RNIB Advisor) says: if you have a small transparent plastic tube, perhaps the packaging from a tooth brush, you can turn it into an interesting toy for a child with partial sight, but only give it to one who will have no desire to eat the contents! Put a few tiny buttons and some sequins inside the tube and fix the ends in place with Sellotape. The sequins catch the light and add sparkle which some children find easier to see than a matt colour.

Shirley also says: interesting toys do not only come from a toy shop. Many unusual, but exciting playthings can be found in unlikely places like the ironmongers, or a joke shop. Look for unusual items in catalogues from mail order firms selling Christmas 'stocking fillers' and search for Webb Ivory electronic toys such as cards that open and play 'Happy Birthday'.

Lilli Nielson (Advisor for Visually Handicapped Children) says: now and then add some aromatic and substantial fruit or vegetables to the child's toy box. Oranges, lemons, brussels sprouts or a parsnip would be a good choice.

A Helpful Colour Scheme for Young Children with Partial Sight

Mme Schneider,
Teacher of Visually
 Handicapped Children,
Switzerland

The colours most parents choose for a baby's nursery are usually pale ones – soft pink, powder blue, pale yellow, and lots of white – with perhaps a touch of strong primary colours in a mobile or a frieze. The general effect is soft, gentle and clean which is lovely for a baby with good vision, but for a child with partial sight Mme Schneider suggests a colour scheme using, here and there, large bold stripes or squares of black and white – perhaps for the bed quilt, and certainly for a play mat when the baby begins to play on the floor.

She also makes building blocks from boxes of various sizes, covering them with bold designs of squares or stripes in black and white. She uses the same idea for the covers of beanbags which she makes in quantity, using various fillings like rice, lentils and gravel.

Use a Special Shiny Play Tray

Instant

Mrs Ross,
Toy Library Parent

A little girl with cerebral palsy who also has a visual handicap finds a box with its base covered with a piece of baking foil helps her to *see* her toys, and keep them within reach. The foil is anchored down with double-sided Sellotape. Usually the box contains toys, but sometimes these are exchanged for a few fir cones, or some large stones or shells. For a treat, there might be some jelly or blobs of margarine to eat – these are her special favourites!

Find the Bead

Instant

Freda Kim,
Lekotek Korea,
The Toy Library,
Seoul

All you need for this game is three beads and three cardboard toilet roll tubes (or egg cups) to cover them with. The child puts a bead in each tube. He hides his eyes, while one bead is taken away. He then guesses which tube is the empty one, and lifts it up to check if he is right. When he has guessed correctly, he watches you change the tubes around and tries to remember the new position of the empty tube (rather like 'Spot the Lady'!). Again he chooses and checks his guess. As a further development, he can change the tube around for you to find the empty one.

Little Tumbling Man

Quick

This is a traditional toy sometimes found at craft markets or gift shops. It is a superb tracking toy, and the sight of the little man somersaulting down a slope never fails to excite both children and the adults caring for them! Many people have asked me for the pattern, so here goes . . .

First find a cardboard tube and a marble. The tube can be made from the inside of a toilet roll. In its natural state, this will be too big, so split it open and cut it to size. In length it must end up about 1½ times the diameter of the marble. Reroll the cardboard and stick it together again, making sure the marble will easily go through your new tube. Put the marble in the tube and cover both ends with circles of thin cloth. Stick these in place. Their purpose is to keep the marble safely inside the tube while all the other bits and pieces are attached. Cut out the chest and arms as in the picture. Add the hands and legs, cut from a single thickness of felt, and stitch them in place. (They *can* be stuck, but tend to come apart when all the activity begins.) Make a hole in the middle of the body, *just large enough* to fit snugly round the tube. Smear the lower part of the tube with PVA adhesive before pushing it into the hole, and press the body round it to make sure it is firmly attached. The hat has two parts. One covers the back and top of the head and the other makes the pointed decoration. The back piece should slightly overlap the top of the back of the body,

cover the back and sides of the head, and the cloth circle stuck on earlier. The front piece is triangular and goes across the little man's forehead and a little way round the sides. Be generous with the glue. Add some shoes, a bow tie and a jolly smiling face, and the fun can begin. Of course, the tumbling man needs a sloping surface for his acrobatics. A piece of board covered with felt and propped up on a few books works well; so does an ironing board closed flat, covered with a blanket, and inclined to make the required slope. It is fun to make several men and let them have races, or follow each other down the slope in quick succession.

Materials
- A cardboard tube
- A marble
- Felt in bright strong colours
- PVC adhesive, and felt pens for the face

The Limpet Shell Game

Instant
(once a supply of shells
has been collected)

Paula Campbell

A family was spending a holiday near to a beach which was strewn with limpet shells. The shape and feel of these fascinated the children and they spent a happy time collecting a vast hoard. Like the little boy with his plastic lids who inspired the silhouette shapes game on p. 80, they liked to arrange them in patterns and play with them in different ways, sometimes making them into ponds for their shell gardens or windows for their sand castles. At the end of the day, of course, they were all taken home to be gloated over again.

It often happens that when there is a surfeit of any one thing, someone comes up with a clever idea for making use of it. Paula thought of a quiet and peaceful game which riveted the children's attention on the shells and did wonders for their powers of observation!

Everyone sat around in a circle, and each person received the same number of limpet shells, say seven. The leader chose a shell from her collection and put it in the middle. Everyone searched through their little pile to find the shell which most closely resembled the leader's one. Maybe it was nearly the same colour, or had an irregularity on one side, or it was almost identical in size. (Try to find two limpet shells *exactly* the same, and you will see their problem!) Finally, everyone made their choice and put their shell near to the leader's. She then had the task of weeding them out, one by one, until only the shell she considered to be most like hers remained. The owner of that one glowed with pride – and became the next leader.

I guess the game would be just as satisfactory if stones

or leaves were used, should you not have a supply of limpet shells handy!

See also

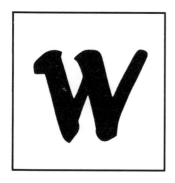

WATER PLAY

Bathtime comes around, some adults think, with monotonous regularity, but for some children this blissful time in the warm water is the highlight of the day. The pleasure is heightened if the time can be extended, and the bath cluttered up with all sorts of oddments to further the cause of happy water play. For a start, cut a washing-up liquid bottle in two, and you immediately have a funnel (the top half turned upside down) and a beaker (the bottom half) to keep filling it with. Poke a few more holes in the funnel half, near the neck, with a skewer or knitting needle and the water will flow out even more dramatically. Put the stopper back in the neck. Now what happens?

To the stock of water toys add a flotilla of boats made from corks cut in half, or walnut shells looking like coracles, or even peanut husks to represent dug-out canoes, and you are all set for an historical adventure.

Pouring water and filling up containers until they nearly sink, stopping at the vital moment when they were waterlogged, but not submerged, then finishing them off with a final slosh — all this was part of the nightly fun in our family. So also was making crude water 'clocks'. A hole was made in the bottom of a yogurt pot. This was weighted slightly with a blob of Plasticine and then put to float in the water. Bathtime could last until it sank. The children became skilful at making very tiny holes! Provide enough containers of different shapes and sizes and the children soon invent their own ways of using them. Providing this does not include tipping the water over the side, and adult supervision is constant, the bath can make an ideal playpen.

A Fishing Game for the Bath

Instant
(This game is not
  suitable for children
  who put things in their
  mouths.)

R.L.

Next bathtime, scatter a few polystyrene chips on the surface of the water, provide your child with a tea strainer and invite him to 'go Fishing'. He must scoop up all the chips, one by one. A few *gentle* waves on the water make the chips bob about, and the job much harder!

Playing at the sink

The best time to indulge in a water frolic at the sink is just before the family wash is consigned to the washing machine, for the grubby towels and sheets can surround the child (on his stool perhaps) and will mop up the worst of the inevitable flooding. A plastic pinny is useful – otherwise the less clothing the child needs to wear, the more likely he is to enjoy himself, and clearing up time will be kept to a minimum if all his clothing does not have to be replaced at the end of playtime! Half fill the sink with luke warm water and pile up a selection of goodies on the draining board. Some of these should float, others sink. Most should be able to contain water in varying amounts, so that they can be used for pouring water from one to the other, filling up and emptying. Popular items are corks of different sizes, bits of polystyrene ceiling tile, a ladle and some spoons (big and little), a tea strainer and plenty of plastic containers of varying shapes and sizes. Provided with all this material, the child will soon find entertaining ways of using it.

Perhaps he will start with the corks and will discover he can swirl them about if he makes eddies by dragging the ladle through the water. Maybe he will fill a large container from a smaller one until it becomes water-logged and finally sinks. Possibly he will use a piece of polystyrene as a raft and will give the smallest container a ride on it. It could be that he will follow the example of the boy in the illustration and press a colander down to the bottom of the sink to fill it in reverse so that the water wells up through the holes, then lift it to make a thunder shower.

If all this sounds rather too damp for your liking, remember that the sink also provides a good place for bubble blowing activities. Look back to p. 34 for some suggestions.

Water play outside

Where space allows, a favourite activity for a hot day is playing with the hose pipe. The next best thing is a paddling pool or a large bowl of water. As well as ordinary water play, these can provide the ammunition for water pistol fights, using *small* washing-up liquid bottles. Children in wheelchairs can join in the fun by nursing a bowl of water and flicking it with a spoon used like a catapult. With practise, they can develop a deadly aim. I speak from experience!

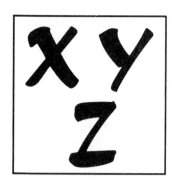

XTRA ODDS AND ENDS!

Make Your Own Magic Pad

Very Quick

Alison Wisbeach,
Head Occupational Therapist,
The Wolfson Centre

This is a 'do it yourself' version of the magic pads that are available from toy shops and stationers. Children love them because of the 'Now you see it – Now you don't' element. Presumably this is the reason for the word 'Magic' in their name. Adults find them handy for writing messages or shopping lists, because they can be easily erased and used over and over again. If you make your own, you can make it a more generous size than the commercial version, and you can create one at any time, providing you have the materials handy, and the chances are your child will be delighted. If he cannot manage to draw yet, he will enjoy watching you make the pictures and helping you to make them disappear.

Make the backing for the pad with a piece of cardboard. Cover this with carbon paper, carbon side up, and keep it in place with Sellotape. The next layer is a covering of greaseproof paper, and on top of that goes the final one of Cellophane or a *thin* sheet of clear plastic. These two layers are attached to the cardboard at the top only. As you draw or write on the pad, the carbon paper is pressed onto the greaseproof. To erase your work, simply lift up the top two layers to stop them sticking to the carbon.

Sorting in an Egg Box

Instant

R.L.

If you want to provide an instant sorting tray at the lowest possible cost, i.e. for free!, use a plastic or cardboard egg box from the grocer. If you want a stronger version, visit a shop that sells camping equipment and buy the same thing in strong, brightly-coloured plastic. The little sections are ideal for sorting shells, pasta, beads, buttons etc.

In a class of slow learners, a small group of children

was busy sorting small plastic pegs into containers according to their colours. One boy was colour blind and could not take part in this activity with any likelihood of success. For him, a cardboard egg box was supplied, and alternate recesses were quickly coloured black with a marker pen, and the others were left white. He managed to select all the black pegs from the pile and only occasionally made a mistake in his choice of the white ones.

Xtra Strong Scrap-books
Credit Card wallets have a firm binding, and the pockets too are reasonably child-resistant! Loaded with cut-down photographs or small pictures cut from magazines, they make attractive individual books for small hands. They are pocket-sized and suitable for the school coach or other journeys. It is easy to change the pictures as the occasion demands – perhaps a new collection after a holiday or on the child's birthday.

Photograph albums – the kind with self-adhesive pages – also make excellent scrap-books. The pages are thick, and some children who are unable to turn a paper page, find they can manage these. If the transparent covering sheets tend to ruck up, fix them across the corners and in the middle of the side edge with small pieces of masking tape, which you can peel off when you want to change the picture. Otherwise, you can permanently fix them down with a binding of Sellotape.

Part III

APPENDICES

BOOKS

BOOKS ABOUT HANDICAP

I Have a Mental Handicap
Althea Greenwood Press 1987
    A book for children.

Music Therapy for the Autistic Child
Juliette Alvin OUP 1978

The Child With Spina Bifida
E. Anderson and B. Spain Methuen 1977

Care of the Handicapped Child
John Apley Heinemann 1978

Making Our Way
ASBAH, 22 Upper Woburn Place, London,
WC1H, 0EP.
Tel: 071 388 1382
    Individual experiences of young people with
    spina bifida and hydrocephalus.

Dibs in Search of Self
Virginia Axline Penguin 1964
    An absorbing account of a child's sessions
    with his play therapist.

The Hyperactive Child. What the Family Can Do
B. Baines and I. Colquhoun Thorsons 1984

Care to Help
Freddy Bloom John Clare Books 1980

In Touch
BBC Publications, P.O. Box 234, London, SE1
3TH.
    Aid and Services for Blind and Visually
    Handicapped people.

Christopher – A Silent Life
Margaret Brock Bedford Square Press 1984
    The biography of a deaf/blind boy written by
    his mother.

The Other Side of Profound Handicap
Pat Brundell Macmillan 1986
    Deals in a most compassionate and practical
    manner with caring for both children and
    adults. Many excellent practical suggestions
    for activities and play.

Helping Your Handicapped Child
Janet Carr Penguin 1985

MORE PLAY HELPS

Easy to Make Aids for your Handicapped Child
Don Caston Souvenir Press, Human Horizons
Series 1981

*The Directory of Organisations for Deaf and Hard
of Hearing*
Charities Aid Foundation, 48 Pembury Road,
Tonbridge, Kent, TA9 2JD.

Helping Your Handicapped Baby
Chris Cunningham and Patricia Sloper Souvenir
Press, Human Horizons Series 1978

Directory for the Disabled
A. Darnborough and D. Kinrade Woodhead-
Faulkner 1984
Available from booksellers and RADAR,
25 Mortimer Street, London, W1N 8AB.
  A handbook of information and opportunities
  for disabled people.

How to Raise a Blind Child
A guide for parents of blind children and those
who work with blind preschool children.
Dorothy Fichtner Christoffel Blindenmission,
Bensheim 1979
Available here from JAG Enterprises, Brookfield,
High Road, Swilland, Ipswich, IP6 QLP.
Tel: 0473 85480
  Suitable for children in all parts of the world;
  beautifully and plentifully illustrated; practical.

*Handling the Young Cerebral Palsied Child at
Home*
Nancie R. Finnie Heinemann Medical 1974

The Deaf/Blind Baby
Peggy Freeman Heinemann Medical 1985
  Very comprehensive.

Speak With My Hands
The Communication of Deaf-Blind Mentally-
retarded Children
Barbro Göras (Project Leader, Jane Brodin)
Available from Handikappinstitutet, Box 303,
16126, Bromma, Sweden. Order No. 7307.
  Descriptions of three children, Anders 5, Anna
  3, Johan 9 and the programmes devised for
  them.

Your Child in an Immobilising Plaster
Angela Greenwood, NAWCH, 7 Exton Street,
London, SE1 8UE.
  Excellent booklet on how to cope with this

situation. Written by a mother who had both
her daughters in plaster at the same time.
Nursing advice, tips on daily management and
many suggestions for suitable toys and
activities for different ages.

Snoezelen – Another World
Jan Hulsegge and Ad Verheul Rompa 1987
A Practical Book of Sensory Experience
Environment for the Mentally Handicapped
  An absorbing book, full of good ideas. Many
  can be adapted to less ambitious projects.

Behaviour Problems in Handicapped Children
The Beech Tree House Approach.
Malcolm C. Jones Souvenir Press, Human
Horizons Series 1983
  Special features of the building-techniques of
  behaviour modification – round the clock!

Starting Off
Establishing Play and Communication in the
Handicapped Child
C. Keirnan, R. Jordan, and C. Saunders
Souvenir Press, Human Horizons Series 1978

Don't Forget Tom
Hanne Larson A. & C. Black 1974
  A children's story about a mentally
  handicapped boy.

Let's Talk
Roy McConkey and Penny Price Souvenir Press,
Human Horizons Series 1986

Help for Dyslexic Children
T. R. Miles and Elaine Miles Methuen 1983

Help Starts Here
Available from National Children's Bureau,
8 Wakley Street, London, EC1V 7QE.

Therapy in Music for the Handicapped Child
Paul Nordoff and Clive Robbins Victor Gollancz
1985
  More for music specialists.

Children of Silence
Kathy Robinson Gollancz 1987
  The story of Sarah and Joanne's triumph over
  deafness.

One Step at a Time
RNIB Education Department 1982
  Useful booklet. Mainly about attitudes and

daily care, but some paragraphs on toys and play.

I Have a Sister. My Sister is Deaf
Jeanne Whitehouse Harper and Row 1977
   For Children aged 5–8.

If You Knew Nicky
Pearl M. Wilson and Sandra Irving Angus and Robertson 1983
   Nicky is autistic

Autistic Children
A Guide for Parents.
Lorna Wing Constable 1980

Living With a Hyperactive Child
M. Wood Souvenir Press, Human Horizons Series 1984

Multiply Handicapped Children
Rosalind Wyman Souvenir Press, Human Horizons Series 1986

BOOKS ABOUT PLAY AND ACTIVITIES

Music for the Handicapped Child 2nd edn. OUP 1976
Juliette Alvin

The Usborne Children's Songbook
With Music for Piano, Recorder and Guitar
Heather Amery Usborne Publishing Ltd. 1988

Swimming for the Disabled
Association of Swimming Therapy
Tree Tops, Swan Hill, Ellesmere, Shropshire, SY12 0LZ.
Tel: 069 171 3542

Puppetry for Mentally Handicapped People
Caroline Astell-Burt Souvenir Press, Human Horizons Series 1981

Art Activities for the Mentally Handicapped
Sally M. Atack Souvenir Press, Human Horizons Series 1980

They Can Make Music
P. Bailey OUP 1973

Home Made Aids for Handicapped People
British Red Cross Society, Supply Department, 4 Grosvenor Crescent, London, SW1 7EQ.
Tel: 071 235 5454

Easy to Make Toys for your Handicapped Child
Don Caston Souvenir Press, Human Horizons Series 1983

The Countryside and Wildlife for Disabled People
Anthony Chapman
Available from RADAR, 25 Mortimer Street, London, W1N 8AB.

Gardening is for Everyone
A. Cloet and Chris Underhill Souvenir Press, Human Horizons Series 1982

Out of Doors with Handicapped People
Mike Cotton Souvenir Press, Human Horizons Series 1981

Outdoor Adventure for Handicapped People
Mike Cotton Souvenir Press, Human Horizons Series 1983

Let's Join In
D. Jeffree and S. Cheseldine Souvenir Press, Human Horizons Series 1984

Let Me Play
D. Jeffree, R. McConkey and S. Hewson
Souvenir Press, Human Horizons Series 1977

Mark's Wheelchair Adventures
Camilla Jessel Methuen Children's Books 1987
   A children's story about a boy with spina bifida.

Knitting and Crochet with One Hand
Mary Konior 1986
Available from Philip and Tracey Ltd., North Way, Andover, Hants, SP10 5BA.
Tel: 0264 332171
   Written for older people who have lost the use of one arm, but could be equally helpful to teenagers in the same situation.

Let's Make Toys
R. McConkey and D. Jeffree Souvenir Press, Human Horizons Series 1981
   Don't be put off by the rather unrealistic times

given to make each toy. The material is good, but may take longer than estimated!

Make it Simple
Easy to Make Toys for Handicapped Children
Susie Mitchell and Carol Ouvry 1985
Available from Carol Ouvry, 2 Rotherwood Road, Putney, London, SW15 1JZ.
  Nineteen ideas. Noisemakers, mobiles, tracking toys etc. Each on a separate sheet in a plastic wallet.

Toys and Playthings
J. Newson and E. Newson Penguin 1979

PHAB Startakit
For those who wish to start a PHAB Club
PHAB, (Physically Handicapped and Able Bodied), Tavistock House North, Tavistock Square, London, WC1H 9HX.
Tel: 071 388 1963

Playtrac Leaflets
On Dance and Drama Activities, Messy Play, Art Activities, Parachute Games, A Brief Introduction to Augmented Mothering, Book List.
Available from Playtrac, Harperbury Hospital, Harper Lane, Shenley, Nr Radlett, Herts, WD7 9HQ.

Guidelines for Playgroups with a Handicapped Child
PPA Publications, *see* p. 192

Toys and Play for the Handicapped Child
Barbara Riddick Croom Helm 1982
  Lists of toys now partly out of date, but the general ideas are excellent.

Making Music with the Young Handicapped Child
Elaine Streeter Music Therapy Publications 1983
  Useful little leaflet. Good for Mums.

Adventure Play with Handicapped Children
Allen Sutherland and Paul Soames Souvenir Press, Human Horizons Series 1984

Music for Living
Enriching the Lives of Profoundly Mentally Handicapped People
Miriam Wood BIMH 1982

Music for Mentally Handicapped People
Miriam Wood Souvenir Press, Human Horizons Series 1983

Finger Play Books

Ride a Cock Horse
Knee-jogging Rhymes, Patting Songs and Lullabies
Ian Beck and Sarah Williams OUP 1988

Finger Plays and Rhymes
Harrow Preschool Playgroups Association
Available from PPA, *see* p. 192

This Little Puffin
Elizabeth Matterson Puffin Books 1969
  A classic for rhymes and finger plays.

The Puffin Book of Nursery Rhymes
I. Opie and P. Opie Puffin Books 1963

Round and Round the Garden
Play Rhymes for Young Children
Sarah Williams OUP 1986

Word Play – Finger Play
More Word Play – Finger Play
Action Rhymes 1985
Available from PPA, *see* p. 192

BOOKS AND LEAFLETS AVAILABLE FROM *PLAY MATTERS*

Address:
National Toy Libraries Association,
68 Churchway,
London, NW1 1LT
Tel: 071 387 9592

For Busy Hands
F. Van de Bos
  Many excellent play and doodle panels that can be fixed firmly to the wall.

Active Worksheets
  Working drawings for many toys and aids.

Look and Touch
Play Activities and Toys for Children with Visual Impairment
L. Clunies Ross, H. Dawe, D. Gaseley, J. Hooper and J. Williams.

Ready to Play
In the Bath, Going to Bed, Time to Eat, Getting Dressed, Out and About, Cooking and Cleaning, Toilet Training, Having a Holiday, Time to Play.
D. Davies, H. Dawe, J. Cooper and M. Red.

Hear and Say
S. Knowles and K. Mogford
  For children with a language delay caused by deafness or other reasons.

Play Helps
Toys and Activities for Children with Special Needs
Roma Lear Heinemann Medical 1986

Mucky Play
K. Mogford

Toy Care

I Can Use My Hands
Alison Wisbeach
  Shows how the use of the hand develops normally and suggests bought toys to help at every stage.

Positions for Play
Alison Wisbeach

TOY MANUFACTURERS AND DISTRIBUTORS

Aidis Trust,
Ladbourne Farmhouse, Ladbourne, Gillingham, Dorset.
Tel: 074 76 2256
  For touch switch toys

E. J Arnold & Son Ltd.,
Butterley Street, Leeds, LS10 1AX.
Tel: 0532 432333
  Educational Suppliers

Mike Ayres,
1 Bury Lane, Stanton, Bury St Edmunds, Suffolk, IP31 2DF.
Tel: 0359 51551/51418
  Consultant Play Equipment Designer

The Birds,
9 Kingsford Street, London, NW5 4JY.
Tel: 071 485 3420
  Large flying birds to hang up; also some original sound mobiles.

The Boots Company PLC (High Street Chemists)
  Have a Healthcare Catalogue at all dispensaries. It includes many non-slip aids, (mats, suction pads etc.) which can be ordered at the shop. About 14 days delivery time.

Caesarcraft Toys,
Ryalls Lane, Cambridge, Glos., GL2 7AT.
Tel: 0453 890 394
  For wooden toys. Handheld Jumping Jacks, Doll's pram with space for brick to weigh it and stop it tipping etc.

Combat Tricycle Co Ltd.,
Telford Industrial Centre, Stafford Park 4, Telford, Shropshire, TF3 3BA.
Tel: 0952 290279

Community Playthings,
Darvell, Robertsbridge, East Sussex, TN32 5DR.
Tel: 0580 880626
  For lovely strong wooden toys; also soft play foam blocks and rolls.

Deron,
Unit 3, Point Pleasant Industrial Estate, Wallsend, Newcastle-upon-Tyne, NE28 6HA.
Tel: 091 263 2981
  Electronic equipment, touch switches for battery driven toys, etc.

Edu-play Toys,
Stephen Lenton and Corrina Orencas, 10 Vestry Street, Leicester, LE1 1WQ.
Tel: 0533 625827
  Well-made strong wooden toys; lovely activity centres; also for bells and diffraction paper.

Escor Toys,
Groveley Road, Christchurch, Dorset, BH23 3RG.
Tel: 0202 485 834
   For a variety of lovely wooden toys with large peg men to fit in holes.

Foamtasia,
BCB Adventure, Unit 2 Rhymney River, Bridge Road, Cardiff, CF3 7AF.
Tel: 0222 464463
   Strong foam-like substance which is very light; pieces poke together to make a Village, Garage, Farm, Train and Station etc.

Four to Eight,
P.O. Box 38, Northgates, Leicester, LE1 9UB.
Tel: 0533 510405
   Toys and educational materials.

James Galt,
Brookfield Road, Cheadle, Cheshire, SK8 2PM.
Tel: 061 428 8511

Haddon Rocking Horses Ltd.,
Station Road, Wallingford, Oxon, OX10 0HX.
Tel: 0491 36165
   Traditional rocking horses and rocking toys. Safety seats.

Halilit UK,
108 Abbey Street, Accrington, BB5 1EE.
Tel: 0254 872 454
   Bright plastic, strong toys; also musical instruments from Israel.

Harrison International,
Arle House, High Street, Meonstoke, Southampton, SO3 1NH.
Tel: 0489 878676
   Recommended for Selecta Spielzeug wooden German toys and Il Leccio wooden toys from Italy.

Hestair Hope,
St Philips Drive, Royston, Nr. Oldham, OL2 6AG.
Tel: 061 633 6611
   Educational Suppliers; also for magnetic tape, blank playing cards, Expoloop.

Oliver Holt,
Treasure Toys Ltd., Atlas House, Chorley Old Road, Bolton.
Tel: 0204 47436
   Lanco Rubber Toys (from Spain) – very light and easy to squeak; obtainable from large stores.

House of Marbles,
Broadmeadow, Teignmouth, South Devon, TQ14 8HA.
Tel: 06267 3534
   Good small games; wonderful range of marbles.

Huntercraft,
Ramsam Stable, Priestlands Lane, Sherborne, Dorset, DT9 4EY.
Tel: 0935 812288
   Educational aids for Special Needs.

ICAN
(Invalid Children's Aid Nationwide),
Allen Graham House, 198 City Road, London, EC1V 2PH.
Tel: 071 250 1612
   For pictures of 100 common words, action pictures, sequenced stories etc.

J. A. G. Enterprises,
Brookfield, Swilland, Ipswich, IP6 9LP.
Tel: 0473 85452
   Low vision aids and advisory service; apparatus, equipment, toys, made to order. Also list of commercial toys for visually handicapped children.

E. J. and M. Law,
9 Pinfold Street, Rugby, Warwickshire, CV21 2JD.
Tel: 0788 61764
   Jigsaws etc., high quality; individual needs can be catered for.

The Little Tykes Company Ltd.,
Unit 9, The Pavilion, Ruscombe Business Park, Twyford, Berks, RG10 9NN.
Tel: 0734 326188
   For large and very strong plastic toys; widely available.

Living and Learning,
Duke Street, Wisbech, Cambridge, PE13 2AE.
Tel: 0945 63441
   Educational games and learning materials.

George Luck,
12 Gastons Lane, Martock, Somerset, TA12 6LN.
Tel: 0935 822 734
   For beautiful *inset* jigsaw puzzles, all sizes; particularly recommended for older children.

M. Y. Sports and Games Ltd.,
154 Wharfdale Road, Tyseley, Birmingham, B11 2DG.
Tel: 021 706 9010

For shuttleball, a very strong game played with checker bats and a giant shuttlecock. Soft balls, for indoor play; Mini Glo footballs; safety dart game – look for these in your local sports shop.

NACRO,
Handicap Aids Workshop, Unit No. 12–9 Sandy Way, Amington Industrial Estate, Tamworth, Staffs, B77 4DS.
Tel: 0827 53032

Nottingham Rehab Ltd.,
17 Ludlow Hill Road, West Bridgford, Nottingham, NG2 6HD.
Tel: 0602 234251
Toys and aids (non-slip mats etc.). Also 'Hal's Pals'; Cabbage Patch disabled dolls; one-legged ski instructor, ballet dancer with hearing aid, blind doll with cane, doll with leg braces, wheelchair athlete.

Optical Fantasies,
Val Corkindale, 16–20 High Street, Ventnor, IOW.
Tel: 0983 852479
For kaleidoscopes of all descriptions, including some which are very small and light.

Pelham Puppets (Marlborough Ltd.),
Collingbourne Ducis, Marlborough, Wilts., SN8 3EH.
Tel: 026 485771
Available in toy shops. Look especially for 'Edwoods' – very simple wooden puppets with only three controls.

Pelikan,
Pelikan Markers, G. H. Smith and Partners, Berechurch Road, Colchester, CO2 7QH.
Tel: 0206 760760
Easily available from graphic shops. Very bright colours for use with overhead projectors.

Peta Scissorcraft Ltd.,
P.O. Box 990, Brentwood, Essex, CM15 8LJ.
Tel: 0277 220495
A range of scissors suitable for a variety of disabilities.

Philip and Tacey Ltd.,
Northway, Andover, Hants., SP10 5BA.
Tel: 0264 332171
Educational Suppliers. Also stockist for 'Knitting and Crochet with One Hand' by Mary Konior, *see* p. 185.

Playwell Toys,
55 Westmeads Road, Whitstable, Kent, CT5 1LW.
Tel: 0227 263649
Strong wooden doll's furniture in proportion for Sindy and Barbie Dolls. Used by Speech Therapists for the 'Derbyshire' Method.

Quest Educational Designs Ltd.,
1 Prince Alfred Street, Gosport, Hants, PO12 1QH.
Tel: 0705 581179
Educational and communication aids. A drawing machine, page turner, pointer boards etc.

Rink Products,
161–163 Loughborough Road, Leicester, LE4 5LR.
Tel: 0533 666382
Excellent table games for older children. Look for 'Junior Shuttle'; 'Rink'; 'Snukatelle'; 'Table Skittles'.

RNIB Educational Supplies,
Education and Leisure Division, 224 Great Portland Street, London, W1N 6AA.
Tel: 071 388 1266
Wide range of equipment and some toys for visually handicapped children.

ROMPA,
P.O. Box 5, Wheatbridge Road, Chesterfield, Derbyshire, S40 2AE.
Tel: 0246 211777
Lovely selection of toys and equipment; also non-slip tray and special scissors.

Slade Colour Games,
John T. Slade, 170 Cambridge Road, Seven Kings, Ilford, Essex, IG3 8NA.
Tel: 081 599 4256
Games for older blind or partially sighted children.

The Special Needs Company Ltd.,
66 Settrington Road, London, SW6 3BA,
Tel: 071 736 8110

Stimulation Frame,
Bitteswell Work Unit, Oaks Industrial Estate, Gilmorton Road, Lutterworth, Leics., LE17 4DE.
Tel: 04555 56263
An adjustable metal frame which is useful for suspending toys within reach of an immobile child.

Suffolk Playworks,
Mick Farrell, Box Farm, Allwood Green, Ricking-hall, Suffolk, IP22 1LU.
Tel: 03598 8844
  Selection of strong, beautifully made play-boxes. Also power-assisted tricycles which are ideal for children whose legs are not strong enough for ordinary trike riding.

Thinking Little,
Dept. 2392–21, Publicity Centre, Hendon Road, Sunderland, SR9 9XZ.
Tel: 091 510 8498
  Particularly good for travel aids for the very young; some toys and cassettes.

The Traditional Music Company Ltd.,
Highfields, Lynn Road, Tilney All Saints, Kings Lynn, Norfolk, PE34 4RU.
Tel: 0945 881 001
  Repairers and manufacturers of traditional stringed instruments, including a lovely single octave zither with the strings spaced well apart.

Urofoam Ltd.,
Radnor Park Trading Estate, Back Lane, Congle-ton, Cheshire, CW12 4XJ.
Tel: 0260 299 049

Foam balls in all colours shapes and sizes. Ideal for indoor use.

WAVES,
Wessex Aids and Visual Equipment Systems, Corscombe, Nr. Dorchester, Dorset, DT2 0NU.
Tel: 093 589 248
  For many magnetic aids, including magnetic tape and bed mirror on a flexible stalk. Magnetic board games, draughts, chess, Nine Men's Morris, Noughts and Crosses. Also a billiard or snooker cue holder for the one-handed player.

Windrush,
55 St Thomas' Street, Oxford, OX1 1JG.
Tel: 0865 250 333
  Large print books – some now with cassettes, so you can read and listen. Also distribute 'Corner-stone', the American large print children's books.

W. R. K. Manufacturing,
Ashfield House, School Road, Fen End, Terrington St John, Wisbech, Cambs.
Tel: 0945 880014
  Bikes, trikes, scooters etc. Individual adap-tations.

ORGANISATIONS

Active,
c/o *Play Matters*, National Toy Libraries Asso-ciation, 68 Churchway, London, NW1 1LT.
Tel: 071 387 9592
  'Active' groups aim to link craftspeople with people who need their special skills. Work sheets for many successful designs available.

AFASIC,
Association for All Speech Impaired Children, Toynbee Hall, 28 Commercial Street, London, E1 6LS.
Tel: 071 247 1497

Arthritis Care,
5 Grosvenor Crescent, London, SW1X 7ER.
Tel: 071 235 0902
  Help with welfare and rehabilitation. Holiday centres. Information and advice. Many branches in UK. Group for young people.

Association for Spina Bifida and Hydrocephalus (ASBAH),
22 Upper Woburn Place, London, WC1H 0EP.
Tel: 071 388 1382
  A welfare service and research organisation. Advice and practical help. Network of field-workers. Care, independence training, activity and vocational courses at residential centre in Yorkshire. Conferences, study days. Bi-monthly magazine LINK. Local associations.

British Deaf Association,
38 Victoria Place, Carlisle, CA1 1HU.
Tel: 0228 48844

British Epilepsy Association,
Anstey House, 40 Hanover Sq., Leeds, LS3 1BE.
Tel: 0532 439393
  Advice and information. Epilepsy Helpline 0345 089599 (calls charged at local rate). Self-help groups. Range of literature including teaching materials for children and information pack.

Brittle Bones Society,
Unit 4, Block 20, Carlunie Road, Dunsinane Industrial Estate, Dundee, DD2 3QT.
Tel: 0382 817771

Communication Aid Centres

1. Musgrave Park Hospital,
   Stockman's Lane, Lisburn Road, Belfast, BT9 7JB.
   Tel: 0232 669501 Ext. 318
   Assessment and advice for all communication handicapped. Display of high and low technology communication equipment.

2. The Wolfson Centre,
   Mecklenburgh Square, London, WC1N 2AP.
   Tel: 071 837 7618
   Multidisciplinary assessment of non-vocal physically handicapped children. Recommendation of appropriate communication system and method of access. Loan library of communication aids. Toy library.

3. Rookwood Hospital,
   Llandaff, Cardiff, CF5 2YN.
   Tel: 0222 566281
   Assessment. Advisory service concerning the provision of alternative and augmentative means of communication.

4. Assistive Communication Aid Centre,
   Speech Therapy Department, Frenchay Hospital, Bristol, BS16 1LE.
   Tel: 0272 701212 Ext. 2151
   Assessment and treatment of patients with severe speech impairment. Information and resource centre. Loans Bank.

5. Communication Aid Centre,
   The Dene Centre, Castle Farm Road, Newcastle-upon-Tyne, NE3 1PH.
   Tel: 091 284 0480
   Assessment. Advice and information. Display and demonstration of communication aids and equipment; software toys. Short-term loan service.

Disabled Living Foundation,
380–384 Harrow Road, London, W9 2HU.
Tel: 071 289 6111
Advice on aids and equipment for adults and children. Leisure.

Dispraxia Trust,
Stella White, 13 Old Hale Way, Hitchin, Herts., SG5 1XY.
Tel: 0462 54986
Put parents and children in contact, locally and nationally. Regular meetings. Newsletter. Aim to promote better diagnostic and treatment facilities and wider understanding of condition.

Down's Syndrome Association,
12–13 Clapham Common Southside, London, SW4 7AA.
Tel: 071 720 0008
Help for people with Down's Syndrome. Many services.

Haemophilia Society,
123 Westminster Bridge Road, London, SE1 7HR.
Tel: 071 928 2020
Leaflets and information. Local support groups.

The Handicapped Adventure Playground Association (HAPA),
Fulham Palace, Bishops Avenue, London, SW9 6EA.
Tel: 071 736 4443
Help and advice on setting up playgroups for the handicapped. Information about play, etc.

MENCAP,
National Society for Mentally Handicapped Children and Adults, 123 Golden Lane, London, EC1Y 0RT.
Tel: 071 253 9433
Headquarters of nation-wide network of support for parents. Excellent bookshop; information; newsletter, regional groups. Central office of Gateway clubs, etc.

National Association for the Welfare of Children in Hospital (NAWCH),
Argyle House, 29–31 Euston Road, London, NW1 2SD.
Tel: 071 833 2041
Supports sick children and their families and works to ensure that health services are planned for them.

National Autistic Society,
276 Willesden Lane, London, NW2 5RB.
Tel: 081 451 1114
Information, book list, suggested toys, etc.

National Children's Bureau,
8 Wakley Street, London, EC1V 7QE.
Tel: 071 278 9441
Library available for reference. List of organis-

ations. Book reading lists on many subjects including child health, adoption and fostering, parenthood, preschool education, disability and illness, drug and solvent abuse, special needs.

National Deaf Children's Society,
45 Hereford Road, London, W2 5AH.
Tel: 071 229 9272
    Information sheets, book lists, advice on education, health, grants and equipment.

National Federation of Gateway Clubs (Youth clubs for teenagers)
c/o MENCAP, 123 Golden Lane, London, EC1Y 0RT.
Tel: 071 253 9433

National Listening Library,
Talking Books for the Handicapped, 12 Lant Street, London, SE1 1QH.
Tel: 071 407 9417
    Small annual subscription. Tapes sent by post.

Partially Sighted Society,
206 Great Portland Street, London, W1N 6AA.
Tel: 071 387 8840

PHAB (Physically Handicapped and Able Bodied) Tavistock House North, Tavistock Square, London, WC1H 9HX.
Tel: 071 388 1963

Play for Life,
1–31B Ipswich Road, Norwich, NR2 2LN.
Tel: 0603 505947
    An organisation for promoting cooperation between parents, teachers and the toy trade and industry to create life-affirming playthings for children. Publish lists of toys and activities for different ages.

Play Matters,
National Toy Libraries Association, 68 Churchway, London, NW1 1LT.
Tel: 071 387 9592
    National organisation for toy libraries throughout the country. Toy libraries loan carefully chosen toys to all children. Some specialise in a wide range of toys for children with special needs. They also provide a befriending and supportive service. *Play Matters* will give details of the nearest toy library and provide information and help to people interested in starting a toy library. Wide range of publications available. *See* Books, p. 186. (SAE appreciated.)

Playtrac,
c/o Harperbury Hospital, Harper Lane, Radlett, Herts., WD7 9H0.
Tel: 0923 854861 Ext. 4385
    Mobile training resource for parents and staff. Play and leisure activities for children and adults with mental handicaps. Displays of play and leisure equipment.

Planet (Play, Leisure Advice Network),
    Also based at Harperbury Hospital (*see* above). Gathers and shares information on play and leisure activities for children and adults with special needs. Advice on equipment. Books and videos.

Pre-school Playgroups Association,
61–63 Kings Cross Road, London, WC1X 9LL.
Tel: 071 833 0991
    Information on Opportunity Groups which include handicapped children. Many leaflets on play.

RNIB (Royal National Institute for the Blind),
224 Great Portland Street, London, W1N 6AA.
Tel: 071 388 1266
    Catalogue of aids and games. Slade games particularly recommended for older children.

RNID (Royal National Institute for the Deaf)
105 Gower Street, London, WC1E 6AH.
Tel: 071 387 8033

Sickle Cell Society,
c/o Brent Community Health Council, 16 High Street, Harlesden, London, NW10 4LX.
Tel: 071 961 7795
    For information and advice.

Spastics Society,
12 Park Crescent, London, W1N 4EQ.
Tel: 071 636 5020
    This society is able to help in a wide variety of ways. Among their helpful leaflets is one that is useful to everyone – *Guide to the Care of Your Child's Mouth,* published by the Dental Department for Children, Guy's Hospital.

Spastics Society Family Service and Assessment Centre,
16 Fitzroy Square, London, W1P 5HC.
Tel: 071 387 9571
    Permanent exhibition of aids, equipment and toys. Publications on play and toys.

Spinal Injuries Association,
76 St James' Lane, London, N10 3DF.
Tel: 081 444 2121
Link scheme for befriending a newly injured person. Care Attendant Agency for temporary carer help. Runs two narrowboats and two mobile homes, (wheelchair accessible) for self-catering holidays. Publications. Local groups around the country.

Sense,
National Deaf/Blind and Rubella Association, 311 Grays Inn Road, London, WC1X 8PT.
Tel: 071 278 1005
Self-help groups; advice; help with claiming allowances; meetings; magazine; home visits. Much useful literature including *A Parents' Guide to the Early Care of a Deaf/Blind Child.*

Voluntary Council for Handicapped Children,
National Children's Bureau, 8 Wakley Street, London, EC1V 7QE.
Tel: 071 278 9441
Help Starts Here and many other publications, including 13 fact sheets for anyone working with handicapped children.

Index

INDEX

INDEX

INDEX

PAGES TO FILL WITH MORE PLAY IDEAS

PAGES TO FILL WITH MORE PLAY IDEAS

PAGES TO FILL WITH MORE PLAY IDEAS

PAGES TO FILL WITH MORE PLAY IDEAS